From Nowhere to Somewhere

Chilton Book Company

Philadelphia / New York / London

FROM
NOWHERE

Jos. Harold Wiley
Kenneth Jeffries
Charles T. Brooker

TO SOMEWHERE

Copyright © 1970 by Chilton Book Company
First Edition
All rights reserved
Published in Philadelphia by Chilton Book Company
and simultaneously in Ontario, Canada,
by Thomas Nelson & Sons, Ltd.
ISBN   0-8019-5569-6
Library of Congress Catalog Card Number 71-123893
Designed by Adrianne Onderdonk Dudden
Manufactured in the United States of America by
Vail-Ballou Press, Inc.

Introduction

We bear an odd responsibility in publishing this book. In these troubled times, black youth is urged to better its lot through violence, non-violence, economic polarization, political grouping and other means as varied as they are persuasive.

The importance of *From Nowhere to Somewhere* is that it presents a practical means for black youth to accomplish its objective . . . an undramatic but eminently workable means that is largely ignored in an era of rhetoric, passion and grand causes.

The three black men who wrote this book were

born in poverty. One grew up in a rural area of the South, another on city streets, and the third in a small town. None of these men had special talents or abilities. They were not writers, artists, athletes or singers—they were average, and millions of black youth can relate to them.

Their accomplishment is a great one; they escaped their background, rose to a middle-income level, established homes and families in an environment of their choice and they enjoy one of the most precious commodities known to civilized man—an acceptable degree of peace, security and genuine happiness.

These men owe an allegiance to their race, particularly in this generation, and their contribution is on the following pages. The attitudes which enabled these men to possess a life undreamed of by many of their contemporaries, and the fact that their beginnings and abilities are identical with those of countless young black people, makes *From Nowhere to Somewhere* one of the most potentially important books we have been privileged to publish.

The Publisher

Jos. Harold Wiley

A BLACK MAN PASSED THIS WAY

our family too much. We had always known poverty inside and out, and the six or seven dollars a week my father was able to make driving pickers back and forth to the citrus groves was the only steady income we had before and during the Depression. If there was a Depression, we didn't know it. We'd always lived in it.

By some miracle, my father managed to acquire a seventh-grade education before it was necessary for him to quit school and go to work. Today, of course, it would be madness to expect anything good out of life with so little schooling, but that was another era, and my father was able to cope with those simpler times by using considerable native intelligence. He was articulate, he was exceptionally good with numbers, he was a serious student of the Bible, which constantly improved his reading abilities, and he had a remarkable facility for unraveling and analyzing life in general to pick out the good and bad of it.

My mother had a sixth-grade education and I think there are two pertinent things I can say in regard to her that will give you a very quick and clear picture of what she was like. First, she was never one to mix with the ladies and become involved with anything apart from her home. She stayed home all the time, kept her ten kids busy around the house, knew where they were at all times and made sure we had an interesting, worthwhile time on our own property. And secondly, she is now sixty-five years old and I have never seen her drink so much as a beer. When a man writes about his father and mother you can expect his views to be somewhat subjective. I have kept mine as much to the point as possible, and the reader will have little difficulty sensing the kind of quiet, caring, hard-working parental influence that guided our family—and, in this respect, we had the most fortunate of families.

Food, of course, was the biggest problem. We had all the oranges and grapefruit we wanted, just for the picking, but there's only so much you can do with citrus fruit and a good diet demands vegetables, meat and staples, items not easy to get without money. I remember one day we had just one can of No. 303 spaghetti. Calling upon all her talents and inventiveness, my mother fed twelve of us on it. It was something like the story of the fish and the loaves in the Bible. And then there was the time all we had were a couple of bushels of yams. We had them baked, we had them stewed, we had them boiled, broiled, fried and, for variety, we even had them cut up in a salad and served raw. I think this went on for a couple of days until we reached the point where I think we would have preferred starvation to another yam.

You know, kids today go fishing for the sport in it. We fished for food. There was no joy in it apart from the practical. The same philosophy applied to our vegetable garden. We didn't grow anything just for looks, and every youngster worked in our garden as if his life depended on it. Nobody grumbled about weeding, and long before the vegetables were ready for picking hungry eyes would search the garden in anticipation. Too much sun or too much rain were genuine calamities. If seeds bought with my father's hard-earned wages didn't prosper, it was a hardship of no small proportions. My father came from South Carolina and my mother from Georgia. It seems that people with these credentials automatically have green thumbs and our garden, as wide and as long as every inch of our property would allow, was generally very productive.

One of my older brothers had a remarkable and most useful talent. No matter how hard the rest of us tried, he was the only one who could manage to go out in the early morning, walk through miles and miles of citrus groves, and return home with a burlap bag full of peas. The citrus growers occasionally planted peas around the base of trees and you'd think anybody could go out there and find these peas. Not so. It took a special instinct and Jimmy had it. A hundred times our family waited hungrily for Jimmy to return in the evening with his peas, and to my knowledge he never once let us down. As the title of this chapter points out, we'd often eat Jimmy's peas morning, noon and night, and, unlike the yams, we never grew tired of them.

In the late Thirties, our family managed to qualify for food stamps entitling us to a limited supply of staples and other items free of charge, but these stamps could only be redeemed for food across the tracks in the white area of our locality, a strange and usually hostile world that I knew nothing about, but which really begins my story.

The only point I wanted to make in this first

chapter is that we weren't exactly a wealthy, over-privileged family. Like shoes would have been welcome, but they weren't an absolute necessity, so I went to school barefoot for six years.

2 "The water tastes the same"

If you're black, you'll understand a little of what I'm going to talk about in this chapter. If you're white—a Northern white—I don't think you'll believe one half of what I write. If you're a Southern white, you won't have any trouble testifying to the truth of my words and I leave it to your own conscience and common sense as to whether or not you want these "good old days" to return.

The Negro community in our town was literally across the railroad tracks from the more affluent white community, and Lord help the Negro man who was on the white side of the tracks without a reason acceptable to the authorities. I'd accompany my father and older brothers across the tracks to get food for our stamps, stand around nervously while whites stared at us, and I wouldn't breathe easily again until we were back across the tracks. I was very young at the time, maybe six or seven, and it was my first brush with the world of real and earnest. I wasn't just a little boy. I was a little Negro boy. I had great pride in my father, but these other people looked down on him and talked to him in a manner no Negro man would have dared to even think about.

I recall doctors flatly refusing to treat any Negro, regardless of the emergency or nature of the need, and, I can assure you, a negro husband or a negro father is just as anxious and worried about the health and safety of his family as a white man. Bigotry in the medical profession is nothing short of hellish inhumanity. On one occasion, my mother walked around for several days with a fish bone stuck in her throat before she received medical aid and was sent to bed to recuperate. She might have found a doctor sooner, but when so many of them turn their backs on you, it's understandable that you begin to rely on home remedies and don't waste the time walking three or four miles to a doctor's office.

If our business took us into the white community, there were special doors to use, special places to walk and not to walk. We went to segregated schools and segregated movies. My older sister made the mistake once of drinking from a water fountain labeled "For Whites Only" and was seen by a white man. Told to drink from the "black" fountain, she did so and then remarked: "The water tastes the same."

Bless her.

Later, during World War II, there was a big plaque in the town park on which the names of the service men were hung. The names were put up on the plaque in the order of their induction into the service and my uncle was among the first to go to war. We were very proud of his name being up there, so near the top of the list.

Of course, we weren't allowed to sit in that park.

If all of this sounds like ancient history, I'm happy to say that most of it is. Twenty and thirty years ago, this sort of treatment toward Negroes in the South was standard operating procedure, but it was what I grew up with. If several white boys were walking along the railroad tracks, busting windows and raising hell, the town authorities would take a dim view of it, to be sure, but that was all. However, I remember walking down that railroad track all alone one day, staring curiously at empty boxcars, and being hustled off by the town policeman for being where I wasn't supposed to be. The general feeling that whites had about Negroes—when they bothered to have feelings—was that we were somewhat subhuman. In their minds and hearts, our emotions and needs were not of the human race. We had apparently just climbed down out of the trees and there we were, standing mutely with our arms swinging down around our knees, making grunting noises to express our needs and desires. If we were denied jobs, or if one of our children died because a doctor's psyche wouldn't allow him to treat a Negro, or if we were hungry, or cold, or embarrassed because we had to beg for survival, we were expected to accept it as a chimpanzee might accept it—without feeling or understanding. This was the tone of the times, and many a Negro, degraded beyond his limit to endure it, has taken a dreadful toll on white society during the past few generations.

The South—that churchgoing, homespun, hospitable, "y'all come back again" South—has given millions of Negroes every reason to blow their minds. If there ever was an irrelevant, Neolithic society destined for extinction, it was the South of twenty or thirty years ago.

Such were the facts as I lived them and experienced them and were it not for the good sense of my father and mother, I most certainly would have become a militant in today's society, doing my best to make gray ashes out of those white-porticoed, ante-bellum mansions we would stare at in consummate awe as children. Anytime a man tells you to drink out of a separate water fountain because you're black and you might infect *his fountain*—although he'll let the town drunk share it, if he's white—you've got a fair excuse to be militant.

3 *Will the real Uncle Tom please stand up?*

There's a story in Genesis about angels coming to Abraham and mentioning that they were going to look over the city of Sodom and determine if it needed destroying. Abraham was upset, so he spoke to God and asked God if He would destroy the good people with the bad. For example, if there were fifty righteous people in Sodom, would God destroy it?

God said no . . . that He would spare the entire city for the sake of the fifty righteous people.

Abraham asked the same question in regard to there being forty-five righteous people in the city . . . and then forty . . . thirty . . . twenty . . . even ten.

And God said He would spare the entire city for the sake of even ten righteous people.

There's a peculiar moral for all black Americans in that story, because there isn't one of us who doesn't know white men we sincerely respect and sometimes even love as brothers. And, for all its ills, most black men love this country, its *stated* freedoms and its opportunities. There is a lot of bad in this nation, in both North and South, but there is also a tremendous amount of good. For every doctor who would not treat my mother, there was a doctor who would. I won't say that for every white southerner who insisted I walk on a certain side of the street there was another one who treated me as an equal, but there were many who did feel that way, and proved it openly, and nothing on God's earth could compel me to put all these people together and wreck their lives.

My father had no room in his life for sweeping generalities. He would never say, "White men are bigoted." He would say: "*That* white man is bigoted." And for every time he clenched his fist in frustration or anger, he would open it in friendship to a white man who had helped him. He noted the difference and he made sure

I noted the difference and filed it away in my heart and mind.

The last thing my father wanted any of us to do was to accept the intolerable social conditions under which we lived. But, if we attempted to change them in a violent manner, we would destroy the good with the bad, our friends with our enemies, and that would lay a burden on our consciences that no sane or compassionate black man could bear. There was also a very excellent likelihood that, living in a predominantly white nation, militant action, regardless of how it appealed to our passions or how dramatic and successful it might be initially, would be met by overwhelming force and completely polarize blacks and whites. This might seem just grand to some blacks, but the practicality of separate white and black camps within one nation is absurd. Blacks need whites and whites need blacks, if not for economic and functional reasons, then certainly for moral reasons. By and large, whites don't initiate the movements and philosophies which bring the black and white races together. It is left to the blacks to do this and the challenge—and the moral victory—may be the greatest in mankind's history. I, for one, have no intention of discarding that bright hope for our race just because I happen to be angry or frustrated and want to lash out at the first white man I see.

Exposed to classical bigotry throughout my youth, I learned an interesting lesson which may not have occurred to many black people. In my opinion, the mind of the bigot can't be changed—and I frankly don't think it's important to change it. True bigotry is ingrown, like a toenail. The lower the mentality, the more likely the bigotry, and eventually, like Dutch Elm disease, it should die out. The white minds that need to be changed belong to those who have good hearts and good brains, but are isolated from the reality of black problems and suffering. There are millions of whites in America who, if they *understood* the conditions under which some blacks live, would instantly devote a large portion of their talents toward making brotherhood a reality.

It was this kind of thinking my father and mother instilled in me—perhaps not so directly or forcefully as I have written—but it was at the heart of their philosophy. Education, they would say, is the major armor you need to convince people of truths they've never dreamed of. If you want to change a businessman's mind about hiring Negroes, you don't wreck his store. You go to him on the same intellectual level he's on and you convince him it's good business to hire Negroes. He may not agree, but at least reasonable communication has been established and maybe the next Negro to talk to him in the same way will finally enable the businessman to see the light.

With viewpoints like this, you can imagine how strongly my family felt about education. Even if we'd wanted to, it would have been impossible for any of the ten children in our family to voluntarily leave school. My father would have literally dragged us to the schoolhouse. If our meals were lean, they were lean. If our house leaked, it leaked. We would bring in what money we could from after-school jobs, but it was better in my parents' eyes to have skimpy meals and leaking roofs than uneducated children.

My father passed up a lot of other items we needed in order to buy us a good history book now and then. Everything at our little school was cast off from the white schools and my father saw to it we occasionally got a first-rate textbook. He had to buy it, and maybe it was because of this sort of expenditure that we had that can of No. 303 spaghetti I told you about. Education for the kids was first, and no doubt or argument about it.

I know it hurt my father's pride to accept used clothing and gifts of food from whites, but it would have hurt him more if he'd rejected these essential items and had to interrupt our education and send us out to work to help support the family. He worked hard, sometimes complaining of cramps, and a hundred mornings —or maybe ten thousand mornings—I'd watch him leave home under a blazing Florida sun, carrying a jug of water in a burlap bag to keep it cool. At night he'd return home, hurting, and maybe he'd made a dollar or a dollar and a quarter for his day's work.

It took great strength of character—almost super-human—to keep from sending a bunch of healthy kids out to work to improve our miserable conditions—but he would have rather died, literally died, than taken one of us out of the only place that would give us a chance for a better life—that stinking, run-down, one-room schoolhouse.

No, he wouldn't rock the boat and antagonize too many whites. Yes, he asked us to be thankful for what little we had. And, yes, he said to put up with the injustice and the bigotry and the frustration so that our stable life could continue until we had enough brains, and enough schooling and enough understanding to go out in the world and change it the right way.

Some blacks would call him an Uncle Tom.

But, as I live and as I breathe, no Negro who ever existed was further from being an Uncle Tom than my father. In his philosophy lay the path to a whole new universe for Negroes—a universe never dreamed of by Uncle Tom.

He gave us what he had, and it was enough to assure a decent life for ten children—a life light-years away from anything we'd ever experienced.

And along the way, because we were educated and sensible, everyone of us helped communicate the true story of the black man to people who didn't understand.

4 Mr. Black

My mother's father worked on a cotton plantation in Georgia in the early 1900's. For some reason, the plantation owner assumed, one afternoon, that my grandfather needed a flogging, so he and several other white men rode up to my grandfather's house on horseback and announced their intention.

As the plantation owner, riding crop in hand, started to step down from his horse, my grandfather picked up one of the sharp hoes he used for chopping cotton and told the men that he was too old to be flogged and, more important, this was *his* house and property and if the plantation owner even stepped on it, he would have his head split open by the hoe.

The men rode away—and so did my grandfather, because the whites would have come back in a large group and killed him by nightfall. The next reported residence of my grandfather was across the state line in Florida where our family took root.

As I entered my teen-age years, with all of the mental and emotional changes that come at that time, you can understand that I thought of my grandfather as a hero. He had resisted injustice in a dramatic way, made his stand and then vanished into the night to start a new life for himself. It was hard to rationalize such a glorious moment in my family's past with my part-time job as a subservient shoeshine boy in a white barbershop.

One of my steady customers was the town policeman—the only policeman for both the white and Negro districts. This policeman was particularly hard on Negroes and I suspect he spent 80 percent of his time in the Negro district. Negro children would automatically run away when they spotted this man's car, and it was particularly galling to me to have to shine this man's shoes. It wasn't any more pleasing to me to shine the shoes of certain other white men in town who just got up and walked away from my stand without paying— my first encounter with mild exploitation. And I didn't much care for being jeered at by white kids and having my shoeshine box kicked over, either. As nice as that barber was to me—and that is the truth—it was also tacitly "understood" that I was privileged to just be in the white section of town and shining shoes in such a busy location. If I raised a ruckus, not only would I lose my job, but I would be known as an uppity nigger kid and there would be a good chance my family would have its credit cut off by white merchants or that my father would find it even more difficult to find local work. The whites sort of had the Negroes coming and going in those days.

That barbershop, of course, was strictly for white customers, and so was the drinking fountain at the rear of the store. As a consequence, I spent a lot of my earnings on soda pop, and it occurred to me that soda pop companies had it "made" in the South. As long as they could keep black people from drinking water as conveniently as white people, the soda pop business was bound to succeed. Somehow, it didn't strike me as an example of the inspiring American business methods I'd read about in my schoolbooks.

Over all these growing frustrations, however, was the calming influence of my mother and father. There was simply nothing I could do about the situations I encountered, unless I was willing to give up my future and the chance to really do something about these conditions in later years. Getting angry and making Page One news at that time would have been senseless. Also, the family was prospering a little better, an education for all the children seemed highly probable, and this was just not the time to wreck everything in a fit of teen-age passion. I was an angry young man, all right, and my father knew it. "If you're really angry," he said, or words to that effect, "get some learning and then fight for your rights in a way that will earn respect and get results. Don't fight about the water fountain. Get some brains in your head and then you can help us Negroes get out of the *whole* miserable situation."

Our family moved to a larger house while I was shining shoes and we had room in the yard for some chickens and pigs as well as a large vegetable garden. I remember we got our milk from a neighbor and made our own butter. We also made our own soap from the fat of the pigs. My older brothers were all working in part-time jobs, so the financial situation around our home had brightened considerably. These part-time jobs I'm talking about were not as clerks in stores or anything like that, of course. Negroes weren't allowed to do that kind of thing. But we cleaned yards, shined shoes and did whatever was considered to be too lowly for the white youngsters. One of us made the mistake of asking for a job in the post office. "You just buy stamps here, boy," was the quick answer.

And so it went.

I quit my shoeshine job when I was fifteen so that I could make more money working weekends in the local fertilizer factory and working after school in the citrus groves. My work in the groves consisted of climbing up a ladder and filling a canvas bag with ninety pounds of oranges or grapefruit and then climbing back down the ladder and loading the fruit into field crates. I think we got nine cents a crate for grapefruit and twelve or thirteen cents a crate for oranges. There were some weeks when I would bring home as much as eighteen dollars—a fortune—but working in those citrus groves was the hardest work I'd ever done and I knew for a fact that this was not going to be my lifetime career. If anything cooled my passions down and made me finally realize that I *had* to have an education, it was falling off that ladder a few times with ninety pounds of oranges on top of me. The working conditions were unbelievable, but if a black man didn't have an education, this was about all he could hope for. I'd look at these people, sweating and straining in the groves, some of them with asthma, arthritis and other infirmities, and I understood what my father and mother had been preaching to me for so long. It would take generations of educated Negroes to change such conditions and bring this stock of people out of the groves and out of the factories—and out of shoeshine parlors—into the light of a decent, human environment.

Now, let me tell you about a white man who helped our family for no reason except that he respected my parents and what they were doing for their children. When a family has ten kids running around a town, people get to know them and, in our case, people were aware of how my parents were giving up everything to guarantee our getting a decent education. One white man in particular outdid himself to help. He lent my father money, gave us clothes and food at Christmas and generally—without any ceremony—showed up whenever we were really in need of something important. He made himself available in many ways, and, doing his best not to embarrass my parents with his charity, it could be said that in his own way he was also helping to underwrite and assure our education. His name was William Lockhart. He is one of the ten men in Sodom that Abraham was talking about when God spared the city.

Despite the good intentions and preaching of my parents, bitterness occasionally got the better of some of my brothers during their teen-age years. They deserve credit for turning out as well as they did, particularly Arnie, who is now a plain-clothes detective. It wasn't too long ago that he was given a citation for catching a rapist and two murders—and breaking up a ring of car thieves.

A good example of the kind of thing that can frustrate a black teen-ager happened when my brothers and I were playing baseball for the American Legion. We were all good baseball players, good enough, I think, so that a couple of us could have played professional ball in later years. Anyway, our performance for the American Legion was impressive enough for our team to be invited to the American Legion World Series in Wisconsin. This was a tremendous opportunity for black boys from a little, unknown Florida town.

Opportunity or not, my brothers and I couldn't go because we didn't have enough money to make such a long trip. The maddening part of it was that we were all strong, healthy and as generally well-educated as local white boys our age, but because we were black we couldn't get the higher-paying jobs they had. If we could have worked in any of a hundred different kinds of jobs in the white community, such as in a bank where we could learn about money and how to handle it, or at least how to borrow it and establish a good credit rating, we could have easily found the necessary funds for that exciting trip to Wisconsin. I'm not making excuses for any black youth who steals or goes bad, but this story is an example of the miserable, frustrating little experiences black kids face all the time and which, once in a while, make them want to punch back at the white community.

These, then, were the teen-age years, with rebellion just under the surface in all of us, occasionally erupting, but usually being conditioned by the long-range thinking of our parents who saw something better for us over the balmy Florida horizon.

By keeping the lid on our emotions, my mother and father made us all very conscious of the duty we owed to our black race and by the time I graduated from high school, I knew that my job was to be a black man whom people would respect—not for his muscle, but for his knowledge, for his compassion and for his dealings with other people.

In a sense, I was Mr. Black, and I was determined not only to build a decent life for myself, but to always act in such a way that every white man I met would think more highly of my people and lower his barriers to their progress.

As I look back over the years, it seems to have worked out that way.

5   *An old man on a porch*

He stood there on the porch, half leaning against one of the weatherbeaten two-by-fours that propped up the porch roof and kept it from falling into the Florida dust.

He looked older than he was, but the work in the fields had done that to him . . . and so had a million memories of being called "nigger."

A few weeks earlier, the man on the porch had mortgaged his house, something he would have done years ago, because there were times, many times, when he and his famliy were hungry, but he had waited until now. Because *now* was important. More important than food even.

He shuffled uneasily, looking up the road at his two eldest daughters. They were going to a place he'd only heard about. He didn't know what they'd find when they got there, but for seventeen years he'd worked from daybreak to past nightfall, and now he'd mortgaged his home, to be sure they would go to this place where he, with a seventh-grade education, could never have gone.

His two girls were going to college. "God Almighty, thank you," he said to himself. Then he turned and walked into the house. He had to be back in the fields in an hour.

Does it matter to this story if I tell you that Allene and Thelma, my two older sisters, completed four years of college, received their degrees, and that Allene is now a social worker in New York City and Thelma is a high school teacher in Florida?

Yes, it matters—because they were black, and because this was the South, and because they came from the kind of life they had come from.

And Jimmy, he went to college, too—and there's a funny story about Jimmy. He started college at Jackson State in Mississippi on a football scholarship. You know where he lived while he was at Jackson State? Lynch Street. So help me, that was the name of the street. And after two years in Mississippi he'd had all he could take and got on a bus and came home. After he'd paid his fare and boarded the bus for the ride from Mississippi to Florida, all he had left was eleven cents and a Hershey bar. Like I said, he really wanted to come home. He finished college at Florida A&M and is now the assistant principal at our hometown school in Florida.

You know, all those things my parents told me, and all the advice, and all the patience and responsibility they tried to push into me, so that I could be a good example of the black race, well, you can be sure that all the other kids in the family were told the same things. Take Arnie, for example. He became the detective I told you about in the last chapter. And Wilbert, he's a supervisor at a home for illegitimate children in New York. Eugene, who earned a degree in Political Science, is with the Medicaid program, and Weda is finishing up school to become a registered nurse.

Not a bad testimony to that old black man on the porch, is it . . . the man who wasn't considered civilized enough to walk on a certain side of the street, or human enough to eat at a white lunch counter, or intelligent enough to work as a clerk in a store. I'll tell you something—he sent *ten* kids to college. Not one. Not two or three. *Ten.*

LaVerne is a licensed beautician, Rubin is a master barber, and me . . . well, that's what the rest of this story is about. I just wanted to pause in this brief chapter and say a kind word about the finest parents any man ever had.

White *or* black.

6　A *funny thing happened* on the
way to Korea

I spent one year in college, majoring in Radio Repair, before I was inducted into the Army. In many ways, I looked forward to my induction. It offered a chance to travel, something I'd never done before, and most of the reports I received from friends in the services indicated that there were very few lines drawn because of race.

That may have been so, but I suspect that many of these friends didn't have their basic training in Camp Gordon, Georgia. After my first few days at Camp Gordon, it was my opinion that if there were still a spot in the United States where they would allow the selling of slaves, that spot would have been Camp Gordon. Conditions may have changed since my day, but if you happen to be black and if you happen to be in the Army, and if you just happen to be at Camp Gordon while you're reading this book, I suggest you do so only at midnight, and even then you'd better read by flashlight under your covers. Man, that place isn't real.

I'd had some R.O.T.C. experience in college, so as soon as I arrived at Camp Gordon, all bright-eyed and friendly, my sergeant made me a squad leader. He just looked over my records, saw that I was qualified to be a squad leader, and gave me the job. Great, I thought. I slept in the cadre room and had charge over a good number of men, black and white. *This* was the way things should be.

For a few days, it worked fine. Then, after returning from the drill field one afternoon, I walked into the barracks and there were my clothes, my bed and all my belongings scattered over the barracks hall. There was also a man standing there saying I was to report to a certain officer immediately.

I appeared in front of this officer as quickly as I could, wondering what I had done to deserve such treatment, and was told coldly, and without elaboration, that I was no better than any other peon in the camp, was no longer a squad leader and, by no means, would I ever be allowed to sleep in a cadre room.

Just like that. No explanation. I was black, and this officer couldn't stomach the idea of my having a position of authority.

Was I enraged?

Yes. Here I had gladly gone into the Army, and the first decent thing that that happens to me is vetoed by a white bigot. I remember making a deliberate effort to remind myself that this was just one white man doing this to me, not the Army. "Now, Wiley," I told myself. "Take it easy. You've faced this a million times. This is just one man. Relax. Things will get better."

As I picked up my gear, some white boys walked over and said they were sorry this had happened. They said I knew my job better than anyone else in the barracks and that it was a damned shame this kind of stupid discrimination was still alive.

A couple of these boys were Southern, and it took a little bit of doing for them to say the things they did. I remember thanking my good sense that I hadn't just turned myself off against the whole white race. Collective judgment is an evil—my father had taught me that. Within the space of thirty minutes I had learned the truth of it; one Southern white man had slapped me down and two Southern white men had picked me up.

With that ray of hope inside me—a hope that said things were going to get better—I started to use some of that hard-bought education of mine to learn my rights in the Army. I read the Army Manual almost every day, quoting it to other boys in the barracks, and calling upon it to help me whenever necessary. I can't say it always worked out in a practical sense, like the time I got into a barracks fistfight because some white boys were playing hillbilly music after taps and I asked them to please turn it off—and one of them said, "No nigger is going to tell us what to do." Naturally, when the dust settled, it was me who was restricted to base, Army Manual or not.

But, in general, I earned the respect of my sergeants, most of whom were strict, white and Southern. "You'll make it," they would tell me. One of them even said, "We know things aren't exactly right around here, but you've got an attitude that will see you through."

What he meant by my "attitude" was this: when a job came up that I knew I could do as well, or better, than anyone else, I would step forward, list my qualifications, then step back. Frankly, it had never dawned on many of the men that a black man could be qualified for anything. Just *telling* them made the big difference.

Many times, white soldiers would listen to me talk about something and then come up to me, almost embarrassed, and ask me to tell them about black people. "Is it true that black people eat off the floor?

How come a black man like yourself, with your education, has to work in the fields? Do you really have all those diseases they talk about?"

Sometimes we'd talk for hours on the subject, and it became obvious to me that most of the whites I talked with, Northern or Southern, had decent, open hearts, but simply didn't know anything at all about black people. They believed in myths . . . in total unknowns. I remember one Southern boy saying, "Man, wait 'til I get back home and tell them what you've told me. They won't believe it. I'll probably have to move out of the county!"

As a consequence of these talks, many of us became good buddies—and, once again, I'm including white Southerners in that category. Two boys, particularly, from North Carolina, became my ever-present companions and more than once, when we'd go to a restaurant in the nearby towns, and the waitress would refuse to serve me, these boys, with their North Carolina accents, would loudly protest the injustice of it and all of us would get up and leave.

The barriers, in other words, were coming down. From suspicion to friendship—it's an easy change when reason and understanding prevail.

Because of my background, I made a high score for Signal Corps School. I was the only black man in this particular class and attended the school for thirty-six weeks. It was more important for white people to see *me* in that advanced school than it was for me to be there for anything I might achieve personally. It was another way of demonstrating that, given a chance and equal qualifications, a black man will progress on the same level as a white man. There was very little bigotry evident in that class when I graduated. It's hard for a man to lie to himself about blacks being inferior when he works for thirty-six weeks with a black man who competes with him successfully.

Some of my Northern white friends in the Army had never seen discrimination face to face, and although it's nothing to joke about, their first experience with it is sometimes worth recounting. On one occasion, I accompanied a white Northerner, three or four Puerto Ricans and the North Carolina boys, to a diner in Augusta, Georgia. Augusta was an Army town, we were wearing our uniforms, and although this was deep South, I didn't think my presence in the diner was out of the ordinary under the circumstances.

I should have known better.

The waitress pointed at me and the Puerto Ricans and said she wouldn't serve us. The Puerto Ricans couldn't understand or speak English very well, and, of course, they had never in their lives experienced anything like this.

My Northern friend, of course, was astounded. It was the first time I had ever seen him speechless and I have to admit I was chuckling a little bit. The North Carolina boys went into their usual protest act, apologizing to the Puerto Ricans and me for the whole stupid system in their part of the country. Then my Northern friend came alive, commenting on the fact that Georgia was a least forty years behind modern civilization . . . that if I had a row of ribbons on my chest, it wouldn't make a bit of difference . . . that my Army uniform wasn't even good enough for a hamburger and that I could probably die of starvation on the diner steps for all these people cared. . . .

Somehow we got out of there alive. . . .

When I look back on it, I think those Army days in Georgia were among the most eyeopening I've ever spent. I saw people change before my very eyes, and I saw why they changed—because I had established communication with them.

And I saw myself change, and grow up, and become a better person who recognized the essential decency that lies in the hearts of most men.

That Signal Corps School was also a school of human experiences. I graduated from both and headed for Korea.

7   Breakthrough!

Seattle, Washington, was our port of embarkation for Korea. I was a green, untraveled kid from Florida, had never set foot in a Northern city, and I took the first opportunity to go out with a couple of other fellows to look the city over.

I had no reason to expect anything other than the stares and "unwanted" feeling I had experienced in other towns and, as always, I shut my emotions off as well as I could and was prepared to accept life as I found it.

I was accompanied on my tour of Seattle by two white boys from Northern states and a fellow black man from Los Angeles. As soon as we arrived in town, the white boys headed for a fish-and-chips stand. I hung back a little, not wanting to cause them any embarrassment in case I was told I couldn't eat at this stand. Noticing my hesitation, one of them waved for me to come on over, which I did. I was asked for my order, was served immediately, and I remembered thinking to myself that this was the first time in my life I had gone to a public, white eating place with the distinct feeling that the man behind the counter didn't notice me as anything except a customer. To the white boys, it was nothing. They munched away happily. But, to me, it was absolutely astounding. I'm not sure how my black buddy felt. Being from Los Angeles, which I consider West, not South, he may have been raised in a more liberal area.

But it was the beginning of a major breakthrough for me . . . the knowledge that cities and towns and areas actually existed where men were accepted for what they were. There might be some prejudices hidden away in the hearts of these places, and black would always be black when compared with white—you know, visually noticeable—but gone was that sense of hatred and suspicion.

It was beautiful.

The city was beautiful. The people were beautiful. (We went into the first hotel we saw and arranged for a room for the night—the clerk hardly looked up. On the way into the hotel, we passed a convention room and, seeing our uniforms, the conventioneers' wives asked us in for drinks.)

People would ask us where we were headed . . . they were concerned, really concerned. Skin color was nothing. We went to the movies. We went into restaurants. Not once—not even once—did I sense anything that made me feel uncomfortable.

"This is the way it should be," I thought to myself. "This is the way it should really be." I fell in love with that city—Seattle.

White people have certain things in common with other white people that can never really include blacks. And black people have certain things in common with other black people that can never really include whites. There's nothing wrong with this arrangement. It's natural and to be expected. Once the hatred between the races is gone, and the idiotic barriers and myths are trampled down—once the whole stupid war is over and the philosophy of brotherhood and of a decent existence for everyone takes over its rightful course—blacks would by and large prefer to be with other blacks, and the same goes for the whites. This isn't a separation of the races by any means—because white and black *brothers* can't be separated. They'll live, play and work together without giving it a thought. But there are times when both races need their own kind—perhaps when they're lonely.

Having seen brotherhood at work in Seattle and being in what I could only call a paradise by my standards, I guess maybe I relaxed and began to feel a little lonely. I hadn't seen many black people in the city, so I went up to a newsboy and asked if Seattle had any Negroes.

"Sure," he said. "There's a big Negro community around Jackson and Jefferson Streets."

I admit his answer stopped me for a moment, because this thought flashed through my mind: "Oh, oh —here we go with segregation again."

A friend of mine in Florida had given me the name and telephone number of a black man to contact when I arrived in Seattle, so I telephoned him and he came up right away and took me to his home.

My first question was about his living in a specific section of town.

"I live there by *choice*," he laughed, obviously sensing my concern. "The whole city is open to anyone. I just sort of like it where I am, and so does everyone else. People who are alike just naturally group together. You know that. If you moved to Seattle tomorrow, wouldn't you want to be with us?"

"I guess so," I said, "but I'd also like to take a look around."

He laughed again. "I know blacks who live in the city itself, in the suburbs and out on the surrounding farms. I don't mean to say that we blacks can always get the jobs we want, or that there is genuine brotherhood in every heart, or that some of us don't face discrimination and prejudice once in a while. But compared to the South, this is another world. For each bigot that still survives up here, you'll meet twenty people you'll really like—and it's getting better all the time."

I could tell just by looking at him that he was a happy man—and when I saw his home, and noted his many white friends, and sensed the security and fruitful life that was everywhere in evidence, I agreed with him that this part of the country was a whole new world. It was a world I dreaded leaving and although I have sinced learned that discrimination flourishes in the North as well as the South, Seattle stands out to me as an oasis of brotherhood.

As I was walking up the gangplank to board the ship, a white woman I had never seen before—she was part of a voluntary group that wished soldiers good luck as they shipped out—tapped me on the shoulder and gave me a beautiful bouquet of roses. "Here, take these with you," she said.

I cherished those roses until they died.

8 Finishing up the old life

Only a couple of things that happened in Korea are worth mentioning. Despite fairly rampant segregation in the Army—divisions composed primarily of Negroes or Puerto Ricans were not uncommon, and a preponderance of Negroes were on the front lines—I somehow managed to be recommended for a job as clerk at battalion headquarters.

This wasn't exactly my idea of glory, but my education qualified me for the job and, as my fellow blacks pointed out to me, this was the first time in the history of the battalion a black man had ever had a crack at a job that involved records, promotions and other sensitive material.

So, I took the job, determined to perform to the best of my capabilities and prove to the authorities that the selection of a black man had not been a mistake. I was on trial, so to speak, not just as Joseph H. Wiley, but as Mr. Black—the old story again.

The administrative head of the office was a graduate of Washington & Lee University in Virginia—a white Southern gentleman of the first estate. If the South were full of such men, the South would be magnificent, because not only did he push the color problem aside and accept me as an adult American male with good training and certain useful talents, but he assumed I was intelligent and able to learn things. He talked with me as an equal and, as a consequence, we ran an efficient office and it was not unusual for me to sign his name on papers and duty rosters.

When my tour of duty was over, I was assured of a promotion if I extended my tour another six months. I decided not to do this, but I had made my black man's point, and I'm sure that particular battalion would never hesitate again to put a black man into any job if he were qualified for it.

Slow progress—but progress.

Another thing I remember vividly is being near the front lines with a white Southern boy. When we went to Korea, somebody said the war was over, but you couldn't prove that to anyone who patrolled the front lines and was shot at sporadically by the North Koreans. Men on the line depended on each other for their lives, and here I was, a black, depending on this Southern boy, and he depending upon me.

One night, in the middle of a rainstorm, the batteries for the one flashlight we had went dead. My buddy had been trying to find his toothbrush and he finally gave up in disgust.

"Well, at least I've got mine in my hand," I said, preparing to use it.

"Fine," he said. "Let me use it."

I couldn't even begin to imagine what would have happened if he had suddenly been transported back to his home in the South and had told his family he had lived, eaten and slept with me on the front lines—and had asked to use my toothbrush.

Strange things happen when the pettiness of the world is far away and men need each other and help each other, and I'm certain that the Army, with all its shortcomings and emphasis on combat, has actually helped many men to understand and respect brotherhood. In some small way, they have to grasp it more firmly, and they must carry it back with them to wherever their homes are.

I returned home from Korea via Hawaii and rate our fiftieth state as highly as Seattle. Multiracial association was as common on Hawaii in those days as segregation was in the South, and I thoroughly enjoyed my brief stay there.

When I was discharged from the Army, I had been away from home for three years. My horizons had widened far beyond the little town in which I grew up. I knew I had competed successfully in the white man's world and I had enjoyed many of his comforts and privileges. I wanted more of these things—for myself and for other blacks.

And I knew how to get them.

9 *This is the way it is*

As I sit in my living room, taping the thoughts for this story, I'm in the "somewhere" part of my life. The "nowhere" part is gone, vanished. It was another existence, unreal, something I must have read about somewhere, and yet I know that thousands of young black people are experiencing, right now, many of the privations, frustrations and feelings of hopelessness that I felt in those early years.

Yes, certain things are different today. Today's young blacks are involved in movements started by our elders. They are more aware of their rights. They are more militant. They live in a time when the social order is changing—in a time when many of the old barriers to our progress are being destroyed. This is for the good.

But the times are also more complicated. In my day, the restrictions were physical—walk here, sit there, stay on that side of the tracks, move to the back of the bus, and so on. Today, the restrictions are intellectual. Young blacks see the improvement in the social climate and they want that "good life" out there. They have the freedom to go and get it—but how? Do they organize teen-age gangs and attempt to bargain collectively with a city? Do they advocate violence for even faster improvement—or whatever else they may be after, including separation from the white community? How do they take advantage of the new climate? How do they "make" it? Sometimes, when I walk through a steaming ghetto on a hot summer day, I have a strong feeling the whole black community is poised on a razor's edge. The overwhelming sense I receive is one of frustration. They know about the good things—the clean streets, the quiet neighborhoods, the fresh air, the decent jobs, the safe schools—they know about these things and they know that for the first time all of it can be theirs. But, *how?*

Black men tried to burn Watts to the ground so that the authorities would *have* to give them everything new, and cleaner and better. That's one way it's been tried. Other methods have included going to City Hall, as a group, and demanding that conditions be improved in the ghettos. These approaches require money—a lot of it—and most cities don't include such programs in their list of immediate priorities.

Black, self-help programs are among the most promising methods used to ease the black man into his share of the economy. There are many kinds of self-help programs, such as the Young Great Society in Philadelphia, and the education of young people and job training rate are the most useful. Why? Because the opportunities opened up by thousands of articulate, patient black men and women during the past generation—the singing masses of marchers and nonviolent protestors who walked through the minefields of prejudice and won a large portion of freedom for us all—these new opportunities they've won for us are there, all right, but only education and training will enable us to take advantage of them.

We are freer now than we have ever been—free to compete—and absorbing the necessary skills to do so successfully will be as difficult a struggle as it was to gain a semblance of freedom.

Black youth needs to learn about business—not burning. That is our struggle today.

And how I admire today's youth—both black and white! They are far more compassionate than their elders and brotherhood is a crusade for them. The bigotry of a Wallace, or the violence of a Black Panther—these things are fast becoming passé, far out of date. Discrimination will always exist to some extent, but it is becoming increasingly ridiculous to hear a black man condemn all whites for bigotry and then ride off on his motorcycle to burn down a white man's store. And it is just as idiotic to hear a white man condemn all blacks— including nuclear physicists—as "niggers." These attitudes are the property of maniacs.

And the world knows it. And young people feel it in their bones. The time for the name-calling is gone . . . *gone!* The time for individual effort has arrived. Black or white, the individual can now move ahead on merit and talent and skill.

Learn, soul brother, learn to compete with your brains and your skills and education, and the new freedoms and opportunities which martyrs like Martin Luther King won for you shall be yours.

Amen.

10 "Somewhere"

Maybe you don't want some of the things my family and I have today. I can understand that.

We live in a small town and I work in the Animal Services Department of a pharmaceutical firm. It's a good job, but because I don't mind hard work and insist on steadily advancing our standard of living, I also hold down part-time jobs now and then. Our home is modest, but we are buying it. It's on a quiet, tree-shaded street where my three children aren't mugged or introduced to pot—or worse—on each corner. They

go to a good, private school and every day of their lives
they become more accustomed to a way of life that had
formerly been reserved for white men, exclusively—and
they're learning how to understand that life, cope with
it intelligently, and prosper in it beyond many of their
white contemporaries. (They don't think of it that way
—it's not a game of come-uppance. It's just a fact that
they're good learners, near the top of their classes, and,
hopefully, they will go far.)

But, whether you, personally, prefer a nice apart-
ment in the city to a suburban home, I know that you
want some of the other things we enjoy. You want to
feel you're the master of your own destiny. We feel that.
You want a freedom of choice in everything you do.
We have that. You don't want bill collectors knocking
on your door. We enjoy that freedom. Above all, if
you're like me, you want to know in your heart that
somehow, and in some way, you've helped your black
brothers in their struggle toward light and freedom.
Above all, we feel that deeply. Otherwise, every material gain we enjoy would be utterly meaningless.

When I left the Army, and completed a second
year of college before going off into the business world,
I took with me the conviction that the most important
lack between white and black men was communication—the simple art of direct, reasonable conversation.

And I practiced what I preached—in a laundry
pressing pants, on a road construction job, making my
rounds as an insurance salesman—I never let an opportunity go by to talk with white men and show them,

just by the things I said, that black men can also read, write and think for themselves and are members of the human race. It took extraordinary patience at times— but I will listen to even the rankest bigot if he will listen, in turn, to me, and in this way we both learn. The bigot's hate is diminished. My anger is lessened. And progress, however small, is made by both races. No violence, or militant confrontation will ever accomplish it.

This was Martin Luther King's great wisdom. When he sent those singing masses of marchers down those Southern highways, and they were set upon by dogs, as millions of horrified viewers witnessed on their television sets, he accomplished more for the black man in America than any violent group could even hope for. The Federal Government went into action, attorneys worked free of charge, thousands of young white people —tomorrow's generation—began to make their stand with these blacks. With every march made by King's followers, new laws were made, white philosophies were changed, the conscience of the nation was shaken to pieces.

Love begets love. And Reverend King—a minister of God, first, and a civil rights leader, second—was an earthly saviour to blacks. His achievements will flourish in the generations ahead, and though he made enemies, he made infinitely more friends. Reverend King made inroads into the white establishment that many blacks thought would be impossible. And he did it without raising a fist. His way was the only way that could prosper—the nonviolent way—and, despite the cries of the militants, the Negro in America has made more progress in the last decade than in the previous two hundred years, and by far the greatest part of that progress came about through a saint named Martin Luther King.

It's easy to go from nowhere to nowhere . . . to go down blind alleys in blind rages . . . to light up the horizon with fire . . . to use obscenities in place of the English language. It's easy to be a black George Wallace, overflowing with hate and venom until it becomes a sickness of the soul and destroys the work and dreams of patient black martyrs to whom the entire thinking world pays homage.

It's harder to learn.

It's harder to think.

It's harder to really give a damn, and get off the street corner, and be honest, and be fair, and be willing to work and study and learn how to get to the next job up the ladder.

It's harder to think of oneself as a citizen, rather than as a black citizen. But that is swiftly becoming the true state of affairs in this country.

And the youth who recognizes it, and who considers himself no better, or worse or different than a white youth with similar education and skills, will be the one to progress. And when he encounters discrimination, he should be prepared to prove, by his reasoning, and, yes, by his astonishment and surprise, that he is up against something unbelievable from the dark ages of men's minds. An effort should be made—daily—to help bring about the day when the oppressors will no longer judge us by the color of our skin, but by the content of our character.

The world is yours, brothers. It's a world in which reason plays an ever-increasing role, and you will get out of it just exactly what you decide to put into it.

Lay down those bicycle chains and pick up that history book.

Go somewhere!

Kenneth Jeffries

MY LIFE
AND EASY TIMES

1   *The Jeffries of Lambertville*

Boy Scout membership had fallen on hard times in Lambertville, New Jersey, the little town on the Delaware River where I grew up. Notices had been sent to the schools and churches to recruit youngsters into this most worthy of causes, and I decided to join up with five of my white pals. I was twelve at the time, and almost all of my friends were white, there not being many other colors to choose from in Lambertville in those days.

We borrowed a Boy Scout manual, memorized mottoes about patriotism, brotherhood and decency, and began to dream of helping old ladies across the street and marching in the Fourth of July parades. We saw a proud, glorious future ahead of us—as only twelve-year-olds can envision it—and, when the time came, we showed up for our interview appointment, chewing bubble gum and with eyes and hearts full of Boy Scout lore and tradition. It was a moment of destiny.

I forget the name of the man who interviewed us—this all-American keeper and symbol of the Boy Scout flame—but he opened the interview by looking at the six of us narrowly, then at me specifically, and suggesting it would be a good idea if I found some other colored boys and started a black troop of my own. As closely as I can recall, he said: "I don't believe in salt and pepper mixing."

We were dumbfounded—all six of us. We'd slept at each other's houses, eaten together, worked together and played together—it was like saying that one of the Three Musketeers was unfit company for the other two.

Without a word, the six of us filed out of the room, the American flag flying at half mast in our hearts, and I knew that for the very first time in my life I had experienced prejudice and discrimination. It hurt as nothing has been able to hurt me since.

And it hurt my friends. There wasn't one of them who wouldn't have gladly exchanged his skin for mine at that moment to take the hurt off my back.

Discrimination was a rare experience in my young life, and except for the fact that I *was* black, and became aware of it in minor ways as time progressed, my growing-up years were as average as those of any white boy in a small town, and I entered adult life with the mores and philosophies of small-town America instilled in me. The fact that I was a Negro was incidental. When you think of small-town qualities—the better qualities of former years and a less urbanized America —you think of people who work hard, are generally honest in their dealings, rather straight-laced and conventional, but with warm, friendly attitudes and a built-in dependability when things needed doing. I think I could qualify on these counts, and I saw no difference between myself and the hundreds of other white boys in Lambertville. I had the same dreams, the same hopes, the same outlook on life, the same everything as they did, and we all accepted each other simply and without any qualifications—such as the six of us wanting to sign up for the Boy Scouts together; it was the natural thing to do. We were all buddies, equal and alike.

Martin Luther King had a dream, and part of that dream was the brotherhood of blacks and whites—not the "acceptance" of black people by white people, but a genuine brotherhood—and, although King's dream was national in scope, and even international, I know what he was talking about because I was privileged to experience it at a local level during my formative years. And the important thing about the dream of brotherhood is that, when it truly exists, you are not conscious of it. It ceases to become an issue. It is just there, like air. It's an everyday atmosphere that surrounds you without notice while you put your mind on other matters. It was like that in Lambertville.

My Dad, Albert Jeffries, had been a long-time resident in Lambertville before I was born, the seventh of nine children. He had rented a home on a quiet side street, and, following a tragic fire in which one of the children died, he purchased the foundation and land and rebuilt the house. The memory of the fire stayed with my mother and father until they died, both haunted by the fact that just a single moment's delay might have saved the child that died. There were only two children at the time, and my mother had thrown the first one from an upper story window to my father who was waiting below. With both hands free, he caught the first child easily, but, acting too hastily, my mother threw down the next child before Dad had released the first one. It was necessary for him to catch the second child with one arm, and this caused internal injuries which soon proved fatal.

Except for that tragedy, our home in Lambertville knew a great deal of happiness, and not the least of its many pleasures was the constant squaring off between my mother and father on every conceivable issue. They loved each other dearly, but never were two people more opposite in nature, and more opposed in viewpoint. In many families, this could have caused major troubles. In our family, it was pure Barnum and Bailey and a good time was had by all. The only thing we kids lacked was popcorn and candy as we watched the circus unfold every night.

My mother, for example—and I say this with a twinkle in my eye—would have invented prejudice if it hadn't already existed. If one of us received a lower mark in school than she thought we deserved, she'd say, "Well, that's just because you're colored. I'll have to have a talk with that teacher and straighten him out." Or, if she got to thinking about Dad's paycheck, which was never quite enough to please her, she'd make it clear that his employers were taking advantage of him because he was a Negro. "They see you coming," she'd say. "Just a poor old colored man, they say, and walk all over you." She saw a clear case of discrimination in every incident that happened to us, and I have no doubt that if I applied for a job, with a high school diploma, and the job was given to a white man with a college degree, my mother would automatically figure it was just another example of discrimination against our race.

I remember waiting to board a bus with my mother for a trip to Trenton. There were two lines of people waiting to board; one line was alongside the bus, to the left of the door, and the other line was stretched out across the sidewalk directly in front of the door. I was about ten at the time, and I was probably preoccupied with my ten-year-old thoughts, or watching a dog or something, but my mother claims that the following took place. (I have to say, "claim," because, as I said before, my mother invented prejudice and this always had to be taken into consideration.)

Anyway, the man standing in front of my mother acted as a traffic director, letting people get off the bus, and then letting the people in our line get on the bus. He made the unfortunate mistake of stopping our line right in front of my mother, and letting the other line start to board.

Well, he shouldn't have done this to my mother.

She promptly pulled a hat pin from her hat and gave him a healthy jab you-know-where, and accompanied her attack with some choice phrases, such as: "This isn't down South! You won't do this to me!" And so on.

She continued to address this poor unfortunate all the way from Lambertville to Trenton, and I remember sitting there, embarrassed, wondering if this thing had really taken place as my mother told it.

We had Irish neighbors—lovely, kind people—and they had to learn to cope with my mother as best they could, because if they happened to be out in the yard, and for some reason—any reason—failed to say "hello," or forgot to nod to my mother, this was an instant case of discrimination as far as my mother was concerned. She was conscious of things social and would go into verbal acrobatics about people she didn't want us to associate with, white or black, it didn't matter; her intolerance and prejudice included every shade of mankind.

Alcohol, gambling, wastefulness, stupidity . . . these things were anathema to my mother. Her brother was an alcoholic, and he made the disastrous mistake once—just once—of arriving in our front yard one afternoon bombed out of his mind.

My mother went after him with a broom. She meant business, and my father had to come out and hold her off before she broke the poor man's head. If anything, or anyone, threatened to lower the social level of her family, or cast aspersions on our character, our color, our way of life, or what-have-you—or if these things were even a thought in my mother's mind—watch out world! Right or wrong, true or false, fact or pure invention, when Mother Jeffries got on her war-horse there was hell to pay.

And my father, of course (it fits), was 100 percent the opposite.

His favorite phrase about anyone who had been unfair to him, or us, was: "Pray for him."

"Pray for him?" my mother would say incredulously. "*Pray* for him?" And then it would start. And we kids would pull up our chairs for a ringside seat.

Dad was among the last of a passing generation. He was deeply religious, devoted to the church and to patience, and to love and to infinite tolerance. He didn't drink—which, in my mother's household, was his salvation. He didn't smoke, he didn't swear, and he was married to one woman for forty-nine years and wed to one job for forty-eight years. Though the differences between my mother and father were beyond earthly compromise, life without him was unbearable for my mother and three months after he died she followed him to her own grave.

Dad was of average size, he had an eighth-grade education, he had worked in a factory all of his adult life and he was black—but there was an aura about this man that commanded respect from almost everyone who knew him. The roughest of the men he worked with would lower their voices and guard their language in his presence. To the best of my knowledge, Dad always wore a dress shirt and tie to work and then he would change into laborer's clothes when he arrived at the factory. This caused some resentment among his fellow workers, which, in this case, could legitimately be called prejudice. When Dad arrived for work one morning, he found the following sign painted on a wooden cart: "Take your tie off, nigger."

The only other example of prejudice which I can recall my dad talking about in detail occurred when he was promoted to a position in the factory that gave him supervisory capacity over five white men. Two of the men went to the management of the plant and said they would not work under a Negro. The managers met with my father and the two white men, and one of the managers said: "These two men refuse to work under you, Jeffries. What do you think we ought to do?"

My father did not have an answer, so the manager answered for him.

"I think," said the manager, "that we ought to send these two men up the road. We ought to fire them right now."

The men reconsidered their viewpoint quickly, and, by the skin of their teeth, managed to keep their jobs.

These, then, were the Jeffries of Lambertville . . . eight rambunctious children, a stern, sometimes rampaging mother, but with a mother-hen complex and total devotion to her family—and a wise and compassionate father who always saw good where a mother saw evil and, therefore, gave us all a well-balanced, healthy attitude toward life and other people. We were black, yes, and of course we were conscious of it to varying degrees and in certain situations.

But, if ever a black family grew up in a white community without hangups and prejudices of our own, enabling us to think of ourselves as citizens, rather than black citizens with a host of specialized problems, it was the Jeffries family (momma, the exception).

If I had been born white, there would have been very little difference in my outlook on life, but after I graduated from high school, I was to see and experience things that made me very conscious, indeed, of being a black man. Had it not been for these early days in Lambertville, in which I came to know and understand that the average white man is no different than the average black man in his thoughts, hopes and fears— that we are all, in fact, clumsy, fallible brothers under the skin, seldom feeling the hate and prejudices of which we are accused, and all of us needing to be given the benefit of the doubt by others—my life might have wound up differently.

A couple of years in the South almost made me forget the deeper truths I had learned in Lambertville.

2 *"The tongue is the enemy of the neck"*

The Arabs have a saying: "The tongue is the enemy of the neck."

So true.

Quick judgements, undue suspicion, impatience, intolerance, a touchy temper . . . these things lead to hasty words, and hasty words usually prompt equally hasty words from others. Before we know it, two people who may have been guilty of no more than being unable to express themselves clearly, are suddenly calling each other names and accusing each other of a whole host of evils. No evil may have been in the heart of either person, but they part enemies, despising each other, determined to have a day of reckoning.

There's no doubt that discrimination exists, but much of it, I believe, exists in the mind, and any man looking for discrimination is going to find it, or think he's found it, in everyone he meets. Prejudice, injustice, discrimination . . . these things exist only in the form in which we are willing to accept them. If a white man chooses not to sit next to me in a diner, this is his privilege. I cannot instantly assume the man is discriminating against me. He may have several reasons why he selects another seat. Maybe he wants to eat where he can see out of the window. Or maybe he wants to be nearer the pretty waitress. Or maybe he just prefers to eat alone. Who am I to judge his reasons? Personally, I don't care what his reasons are . . . but I cannot suspiciously label them "discriminatory" unless his actions are clearly discriminatory. That's the difference between guessing and knowing; and people, groups, towns and cities have been torn asunder because of hasty guesses and quick judgements about the motives of the other guy. People—all of us—are so damned awkward when it comes to expressing ourselves, when it comes to doing and saying things that accurately represent the way we feel, that there is a whole world of feeling between what is in our hearts and what we say to our fellow men. It's the *communication* that needs improvement. That fellow who chooses not to sit next to me in the diner, and who bulls himself into a line ahead of me, or seems to look at me narrowly with a suspicious mind may help me change a tire on my car ten minutes later. He'll still look at me the same way, and still be just as awkward in his words and actions, but all of this is just a misreading of what is really in his heart.

It isn't always this way . . . but I have found it to be *almost* always this way. If I wake up in an ornery mood, I'll look for and find discrimination in everyone I meet. If I wake up sane and sensible, trying to understand other people the way I want them to understand me, and refuse to jump to fast conclusions, I am hard put to find anyone who clearly displays prejudice and discrimination.

I'm not just relating to the quiet area in which I grew up. I've been in the ghettos, and in the cities, and I've been in the South. There's no question about discrimination in the South—none at all—and there's no question about it existing in a subtler form in the North. But, on a man-to-man basis, setting aside discriminatory policies laid down by shadowy people in important business, government and social positions—in person-to-person situations, I, for one, have found very little heartfelt discrimination.

The Boy Scout leader I told you about considered my color a fearful and important difference. He didn't know anything about me at all. All he could do was *see* my color. On this basis, oblivious to everything else, he was willing to squash the hopes and sensitivities of a twelve-year-old boy. This was not the policy of the Boy Scouts of America. This was the warped bigotry of one, specific man, and more than one black youngster, stung by such hate, has grown up to loathe all white men and fight them viciously.

The New Jersey State Police gave me my second major experience with discrimination. Again, I think I was about twelve years old. I was Captain of the Safety Patrol at school, and once a year the State Police would invite members of Safety Patrols throughout the state to swim at the State Police swimming pool.

Well, this was a big thing. I remember polishing up my belt, to be as presentable as possible, (after all, I *was* Captain of the Safety Patrol) and I was really impressed when the State Trooper came to the school, all shiny and authoritative in his State Police uniform. The trooper looked at us, and then he pointed to me and asked if I knew how to swim.

"Well, about as much as my buddies," I said.

"Are you a *good* swimmer?" he asked.

"I can keep myself up," I said. "You know, just like the other guys."

"Well, that pool's pretty deep over there," the State Trooper persisted, "and we only want really good swimmers."

I told him again I could swim as well as my pals, but the trooper kept insisting that I had to be an excellent swimmer to go to this pool. It never occurred to me that I was being discriminated against. I took the trooper at face value and figured he just didn't think I was a good enough swimmer—I even started to have doubts about it myself. Maybe I *wasn't* a good enough swimmer.

It wasn't until a few years later, when there was a public issue about the lack of Negroes in the State Police, that it suddenly dawned on me that, by golly, *I had been discriminated against!*

Perhaps the most classic example of discrimination in my young life occurred when I was about fourteen. I was part of a Bugle Corps in Lambertville—the only Negro in it—and we were scheduled to have an outing, a day on the beach at Cape May, New Jersey.

This was a tremendous thrill for me, because, although I had seen the ocean once, at Coney Island, I had never had the chance to really be on the beach and swim in the surf. I was excited beyond the telling of it. This was really a big event, and I was allowed to take a friend, so I took my brother, and that made two of us who couldn't wait to get to Cape May.

I don't have to tell you what happened . . . you already know. My brother and I were not allowed to use the public locker rooms to change into our bathing suits. We went to two locker rooms—the guard at the first one was subtle. He said the lockers were all taken. Okay—so we went to the next locker. The guard at this one laid it on the line to us: "We don't allow no niggers in there. Get out of there!"

My brother cried. I cried.

"Go on," we said to the other white guys with us. "You go ahead and swim. We don't want to swim, anyway."

Then my brother and I walked down the board-walk. We felt lost, and we were afraid to even stop for an ice cream cone or do anything at all. We'd never been away from home very much, and everything seemed strange and threatening. Later, we were told there was a beach for Negroes, but we didn't see it. We just walked around until it was time to go home.

All right, so those were my experiences with discrimination during my youth—isolated instances; sharp, clear, unmistakable. There were others, mostly minor, so trivial, in fact, that recalling them is difficult, although I do remember our school class decided not to go to Washington, D.C., when it was pointed out that I might not be allowed to share hotel rooms with my buddies, eat at certain places, and so on. The whole class said the hell with it and we went to New York instead.

Balancing such incidents against the far better nature in white men that I generally experienced did not take any special effort. There would always be white men who would wish me nothing good, but I found many more who sincerely wished me well. More than anything else, instances of discrimination simply made me aware that, like it or not, my color made me different and people would take different attitudes toward it. This was fact, not just something I wished to think, or not to think. I resented prejudice when I faced it, and I have no intention of excusing those who practice it. By the same token, *I* didn't want to practice it, either, and I knew very well that in most of my dealings with white people there was no prejudice on either side. It would be just as unfair of me to be prejudiced against a man, because he was white, as it is for a white man to be prejudiced against me because I am black. I'd be just as big a bigot, just as intolerant, and just as asinine. That's a fact, not an opinion.

My awareness of being black *did* cause me to be more conscious of my actions and, as I got into my teens with a few unhappy experiences behind me, I know that I was constantly checking my appearance and conduct so as not to call undue attention to myself. In this sense, I was never completely free or relaxed. Our society is primarily white, let's face it, and I acted in such a way that I would avoid incidents and do my best to show prejudiced whites, if there happened to be any of them around, that I was not what they might think I was.

So, that's what it was—an *awareness* of being a Negro, but by no means resenting it or concluding that every white man had the same heart as that Boy Scout leader or that guard at Cape May.

I despise prejudice wherever it is found—in white men or black men—and this is the attitude I carried with me into the Marines, into Korea, and into the South.

3 *The real thing*

Fresh out of high school, the ink hardly dry on my diploma, I went to Trenton to enlist in the Marines.

"Welcome aboard, mister," said the recruiting sergeant, all smiles and sweetness, "here's your application."

So, I filled out the application and handed it back to him.

"Of course, you know," he said, assuming a thoughtful expression—something seldom witnessed on the face of a Marine Sergeant—"you can only be assigned to cook's school, baker's school or to general duty." (General duty, I discovered later, meant carpentry, painting, hauling ammunition boxes or other trivial duties—positively no combat, or technological schools, or any chance for bettering myself or advancing my skills.)

I asked the Sergeant what this rule was all about, and he said he didn't make the rules, and really didn't agree with them (they all put it that way), but this was how matters stood.

Well, nuts to the Marine Corps, so I went home and figured I'd wait for the Army to draft me. During the following year, however, I noticed in the press that the rules about Negroes in the Marine Corps were being altered. I couldn't help but assume that the Marines were running out of white men to get shot up, so they decided to lower the barriers to Negroes. Anyway, I went back, checked out the facts, and, sure enough, the rules had changed, so I enlisted.

A few days later, I got off a train in Beaufort, South Carolina, preparatory to taking a bus over to Parris Island where we were to go through Boot Camp.

Friends, believe me when I say that I was about to undergo the greatest shock of my life. All of a sudden I was in the South, and I really *knew* it. There was no doubt about it, whatsoever.

I had struck up a casual acquaintance with two other Negroes who came from Philadelphia, and while we were waiting for the bus, one of my new-found buddies ventured into a little store that was next to the train station. I think he wanted to buy some candy.

Without exaggeration, you could hear the proprietor of that store for at least a mile as he came out, screaming at my friend: "You got no business coming in here, nigger! Get out of here, nigger! Don't set foot in this store, nigger! Who the hell do you think you are, nigger!" . . . and so on and so on, screaming like a man possessed.

A great silence enveloped everyone who witnessed this mad scene. All of the Marine recruits on our train, white and black, had come from the North and had never in their lives seen anything like this. Eventually the man stopped screaming and went back into his store. It was eerie. You could still hear the echoes of his ravings bouncing off the buildings further down the street. It was a dream . . . a nightmare.

I had been hurt the most during my experience with the Boy Scout leader . . . because it was the first major realization of what discrimination felt like. I was older now, and although this episode didn't hurt as much, I can explain the feeling better. When a Negro unexpectedly comes face to face with the sort of rabid madness I witnessed in South Carolina, the hurt begins in the stomach. He can literally feel it there. It is heavy, soggy, like a lump of bread dough. Then it begins to work its way up, until he feels as if he is going to vomit. Often a cold sweat develops and the hands shake. The feeling is infinitely beyond hurt, beyond embarrassment, beyond anger. It is a feeling of being a block of wood. An absolute nothing. Worse than an animal. It is the most sickening, the most awful feeling a man can have, and I am certain that if every white man could experience it just once, this world, the day after, would be on the verge of brotherhood.

Needless to say, we did not get over that initial shock and hurt; we did only what we could do, and that was to accept it. We were in the Marines. We were not civilians. Had we been civilians, I think we would have joined with the ranks of other Negroes in the South who, through marches, demonstrations and economic boycotts, were beginning to make inroads into this derelict culture.

At Parris Island, on the base, itself, I can say truthfully that I was not conscious of discrimination. Certainly nothing memorable. The drill instructors showed no mercy to black or white; we were *all* discriminated against! I was made a platoon leader, and I enjoyed the toughening up process of boot camp. Off base, however, was always a different story, and I was constantly on the alert for open displays of prejudice, places where I wouldn't be allowed to eat, and so forth. For example, the following incident occurred at a roadside restaurant in North Carolina on my way home from boot camp.

There were enough fellows from the Philadelphia area to warrant our chartering a bus, which we did, and when it stopped at this restaurant, the bus driver told me—and the two other Negroes on the bus—not to go into the restaurant.

"I've talked with the manager," he said. "He's going to feed you, but you can't eat with the rest."

I'm sure the bus driver thought this was a fine gesture on the restaurant manager's part, and I was particularly impressed with the way he said *feed* . . . "he's going to *feed* you." He sounded like I used to sound when I fed my dog—and I made up my mind never to speak to my dog that way again.

So, we followed the bus driver into the back of the restaurant and somebody set up a card table for us in the pantry. Grease, dust and smoke were all over the place. It was filthy. A colored chef prepared our meal and he seemed quite indignant that we were eating in his lousy pantry. He was as bad as the whites.

Somehow, we managed to stuff down our gruel—
we were fortunate it wasn't served in a "Snoopy" dish
and placed on the floor for us to lap up.

You can almost make something like this sound
funny, but it's not funny, not funny at all. One of the
fellows, a big guy from Philadelphia, actually had tears
in his eyes as he ate.

It was the same all over the South . . . experience
after experience. There was no getting away from it.
A hundred times or more I've heard a bus driver say,
"Move to the back of the bus, boy, where you belong."
I remember a sweet, little, old colored lady telling me
to move back, so that I wouldn't upset the system, and
I also remember a bunch of white Northern recruits,
who had finally "had" it, refuse to budge from the
back seat so that the bus driver *had* to let me sit up
front.

If there *was* a funny incident, this was it: I was
stationed in Norfolk, Virginia, and one day, in the middle of a heavy rainstorm, I stepped into a dinky, little
hole-in-the-wall restaurant to wait for a bus. I described
the pantry in the North Carolina restaurant as being
filthy, but this was infinitely dirtier. Cobwebs hung in
the corners, flyspecks were on the unwashed windows,
the upholstery on the three or four stools in front of the
counter was falling out onto a floor that hadn't been
swept since Pearl Harbor day. It was unbelievable.

But it was better than the rain, so, to make my
presence at least profitable to the white proprietor, I

stuck a dime in a soda machine and started to enjoy a Coke.

Without thinking, and keeping one eye out for the bus through the filthy windows, I backed up to one of the stools and *almost* sat down—because I heard such a bloodcurdling scream from the proprietor that I jumped up, wondering what in God's name was happening, and dropped the bottle of soda.

"Don't you sit down on that stool," he screamed. "Don't you sit down on that stool. I'm doing you a favor by letting you drink that soda in here."

I had to laugh—I really had to. Under normal circumstances I wouldn't want to be *seen* in a place like that. And he had the nerve to tell me he was doing *me* a favor!

White Southerners hate white Northerners a lot more than Negroes—that is one thing that impressed me constantly. Never had I heard the term, "damn Yankee," used so repeatedly and with such venom. It seemed as if the Southerners blamed the Northerners for every ill, particularly in regard to integration and other matters pertaining to Negroes—and their wrath was directed toward any and all white Northerners who crossed their paths.

While I was in Korea I made friends with several white men from the Deep South. I was a sergeant in charge of a mine-clearing squad—work that is exceptionally hazardous and brings your men close together for mutual protection—and I found out a few things about Southerners.

First, during many discussions, I never met a Southerner who had actually sat down and discussed segregation with a Negro. They didn't know why segregation existed, or why there were special rules, or how or why the whole system was in operation. A Negro, to these people, was just a thing. They didn't think well of the Negro, nor did they think ill of the Negro. He was just there. He existed.

As a consequence, the Southerners I talked with didn't feel guilty about anything, nor did they feel they owed the Negro anything. The Negro was looked upon as a nonentity; like that "block of wood" I said I felt like when I first arrived in South Carolina.

This policy of limbo for the Negro meant not only that the black man was required to remain apart from the white man, but also that the white man was not to intrude on the Negro's ground. I remember meeting a white friend of mine at a segregated bus depot in Jacksonville, North Carolina. My white friend was from Lambertville—I had grown up with him—and he had actually joined the Marines because I had. Now, at long last, we had managed to make connections.

We were standing on the platform, catching up on the news about each other, when it started to rain. Automatically, I headed for the colored section of the depot —I had finally gotten this segregation business through my head and it had become instinctive.

Naturally, my friend followed, thinking nothing of

it. Well, a nearby white policeman had some different thoughts about it. He was big and burly, with size 13D brogans, and he grabbed my white friend by the collar and said, "You're the kind who makes it hard for us down here. You don't belong in here. If you two want to talk, you talk on the outside." Then he removed my friend, bodily, from the colored section.

In short, there was to be no mixing of the races in the South, and, as I indicated earlier, this classic, white Southerner was a lot angrier at my Northern white friend than at me.

The humiliation visited upon Negroes in the South, during the days I was there, had different effects on different men. I've had black friends who literally went hungry rather than be degraded. I had white friends— many of them—who would not eat at restaurants that wouldn't serve me. I've heard black men swear they were going to return to the South after their service and fight militantly for their depressed and humiliated brothers, and I'm confident that some of them did just that.

Many changes have taken place in the South since my days in the Marines, and I think the one most important lesson the South learned, and that has caused these changes, is that the Southern Negro has immense economic power when it is brought together and channeled wisely. Many Negroes disagree with me, but I believe that Martin Luther King, and other Negro groups that used the great power in peaceful marches and economic boycotts, rather than rely on the quick, all-or-nothing militant confrontation and a quick decision, have used the *only* methods that can seriously and safely alter the Negro's life in the South on a long-range basis.

Despite the screaming segregationists . . . despite the Southern system that degrades the Negro, I am convinced of a very strange thing, but I am very *much* convinced of it.

I believe the South will solve its black/white problems sooner than the North, more permanently than the North, and with absolute sincerity. When they solve it, it will be solved. There is a vicious subtlety in Northern discrimination that is seldom seen in the South. The Southerners are open and honest about their feelings. When they change, they will be equally open and honest about that. There will be no carefully coded job application forms that slyly indicate the applicant is a Negro . . . no sneaky "understandings" in social clubs, businesses, hotels, and so on. And, when the average Southerner begins to realize that the Negro is not a "thing," and that his status as a human being and as a citizen is identical to theirs—when that revelation sweeps into the hearts of Southerners—those hearts will change and they will honor the change.

I think the time is coming when it will be better—far better—for a Negro to live in the South, rather than in the North.

4 *Starting up the ladder*

My experiences in the Marines reinforced the opinions and attitudes I had formed in my youth. I saw no reason to change my viewpoint regarding the essential sameness of all men, black and white, or the one conviction that is central to my entire philosophy—that prejudice is a rare commodity in men and it is essential to give others the benefit of the doubt. I would have to except many Southerners from that philosophy, of course, but, as communication between black and white progresses in the South, I believe that most prejudice will genuinely be wiped away. I am not a crusader, but I saw great promise in Reverend King's peaceful approach to the Negro's problems in the South and I defended it as directly and as articulately as opportunity and situations allowed. It was not a major contribution to the black man's struggle, to be sure, but I felt it was the most sensible and worthwhile that I could make. Each black man wrestles with this problem in his own way, and each must do what he feels is best. I feel I have done, and am doing, my best.

Another attitude that had not changed when I resumed my civilian life was my basic confidence in human nature. I was not—obviously—allied with my fellow blacks who automatically assume the white man is constantly trying to "do him in." Many of my black friends told me that I couldn't get this job, or that job, or be promoted, or make progress. It was nonsense, and I knew it. It was defeatism at its worst. If a Negro offers a decent, prospective white employer the same credentials as a white man . . . if the employer likes these credentials and likes the forthrightness, appearance and other attributes of the Negro applicant, I hold that the Negro has a *better* chance of getting that job than the white man. That is the extent to which I trust the intrinsic good nature of most people; I feel the white man—the decent white man—will do more on behalf of the Negro than he will for whites.

Be that as it may—whether the employer would do more or less for the Negro, and whether you agree or disagree—I knew that if the only thing different about me from white men was the color of my skin, I had little to fear and could plan my future confidently.

It worked exactly that way. If I had been intolerant of white men, if I had "seen" discrimination and prejudice written on every white face, if I had convinced myself that I had no chance in a white society, if I had looked upon the white world with suspicion and intolerance, I have no idea where I might have wound up.

Probably hating everybody, and mostly myself for my stupidity.

I had married during my hitch in the Marines, and when I was discharged I also had a baby to take care of. The first thing I needed was a job, and I found one immediately in the Physical Laboratory (Quality Control) of the paper mill in which my dad had worked. I supplemented my income by beginning a catering service, and then I turned my attention toward buying a home.

The real estate agent I contacted showed me two homes—one practically straddling some railroad tracks, and another one, in the country, that was owned by Negroes. (Perhaps the last battle the Negro will have to fight to gain full citizenship in this country is the one to convince white homeowners that a Negro family in the vicinity does not automatically lower real estate values. You could call this prejudice against the Negro, and, of course, it has been carried to extremes by frightened low- and middle-class homeowners who have actually burned Negro homes in developments. But, generally, in the more civilized areas, there is not hatred or violence of this sort and the problem is strictly a monetary one; the white homeowner is sincerely afraid his home, or his area, will be devalued as a result of having Negro neighbors. I think that such a homeowner has an interesting time wrestling with his conscience. On the one hand, he may be compassionate, open-minded, and sincerely desire brotherhood among all peoples. But if his financial security is threatened, he suddenly finds his philosophies very awkward. It is prejudice against the Negro, yes, but it is also a business decision he must make, and I don't envy the soul-searching he faces. The worst part of it is that the myth—and numerous studies have shown that it is a myth—the myth of property devaluation when Negroes move into a community, particularly in the country or in small towns, is as prevalent among real estate brokers as among homeowners. It's the myth that should be attacked, not the people who believe it and lie awake nights trembling because they think their life savings are suddenly being undermined.)

Anyway, we bought the home in the country. Happily, it was just what we wanted; ten acres, seclusion, woods, fields and low in price. If we had been shown dozens of other homes, this probably would have remained our first choice.

Interestingly enough—just to go back a moment— we found many more properties were available to us than the real estate people thought. They had been injecting their own prejudices into our transactions, and, on one occasion, before buying our country home, we had looked at a lot that I *knew* was for sale to anybody who wanted it. The real estate broker had said the owner had specifically stated this lot was not to be sold to Negroes. The lot was too expensive for us, anyway, but my wife's family knew the wealthy white owner of the lot and we decided to tell her what the broker said.

We did—and she was furious, taking the property out of the broker's hands and tempting us in many ways to buy it.

On still another occasion, after having been told there were no homes available to Negroes in the area, a very prominently social woman, and a true humanitarian, telephoned us and said that she had a lovely home in the middle of town and would sell it to us at the barest possible minimum! It was, indeed, a beautiful home, but, at the very least, it would cost half as much again as we felt we could afford. She was not making a nickel on this house, we knew that, and she even urged us to purchase it as an investment. It was a very wonderful and kind thing for her to do, but it was simply beyond our means. Her name is Mrs. Scull, and I would like her to be remembered in this book.

Mrs. Scull also helped influence the bank to give us the money we needed for our present home. The world needs many more Mrs. Sculls.

Because of the shift-work nature of my job at the paper mill, I managed to come up with a nervous stomach after a couple of years and had to take some time off to recuperate. When I returned to work I found a new and better job waiting for me in the chemistry laboratories. I hadn't known it, but technological research was my field, particularly the experimental end of it. Lacking a college degree, I can only thank Carl Ackerman, Technical Director of the mill, for putting me into this job to start with, and Russ Bowe, the chemist who tucked me under his wing, glad to have me, and taught me patiently and carefully. Both of these men were white.

I left the paper mill with reluctance a few years ago to earn more money and assume more responsibility as a senior technician in an electro-chemistry laboratory. This move would have been difficult, of course, without the help of Messrs. Ackerman and Bowe. In fact, they taught me so much that I think I can say that my knowledge and abilities, again, in the experimental field, are equivalent to those of many men in the industry who have had the very important benefit of a higher formal education.

So much for my formal work. The catering business was growing and it was presenting some interesting problems.

5 Everybody's man, Jeffries

During my four years in high school, I had held a part-time job in a restaurant, and when I graduated from school and joined the Marines I made the statement to my mother that I would never again work in somebody's kitchen. I had no intention of waiting on tables and washing dishes, and I would never be a domestic, or a cook, or somebody's "man."

Well, as it turned out, I became *everybody's* "man." A combination of economics, a growing family, a limited education, experience in the restaurant business, and an uncle who was in the catering business, put me into the catering business, too.

Oddly, I liked it.

I not only liked it, I was good at it. The customers I helped my uncle cater—for parties, weddings, other social events, and so forth—were usually quite wealthy. I enjoyed talking with these people, and they enjoyed talking with me. I paid strict attention to my appearance and bearing, did my job responsibly and pleasantly, and within a short time I found myself in business for myself. My uncle had more business than he could handle, and I think he would agree that I was not competing with him to any serious extent.

Catering, of course, is primarily a weekend and holiday business, and it can become grueling at times. But it is profitable, and, with my wife's help, it supplemented the income from my regular work and I'm glad to say that we managed to pay our mortgage and other bills with satisfying promptness.

Catering, being the social business that it is—preparing and serving foods and drinks to guests in a private home, and usually on a happy family occasion—required more than just a simple do-the-job attitude. In this business, as in everything else in life, I had to develop certain philosophies if I was to progress. Among these philosophies was acceptance of—and amusement at— the simple fact that people enjoy having Negro servants running about. As far as I was concerned, this was fine; it was the basis of my very lucrative and rapidly growing business.

So, naturally, the men I hired to help me were also colored. I taught them the business, emphasizing the necessity for neatness, politeness and, above all, discretion. (I have been asked to write a book on my experiences as a caterer, but I would never think of such a thing. Odd incidents can happen at parties, particularly as the hour grows late, and the cumulative effects of drink begin to take hold, and I—and the people who work for me—studiously avoid seeing, hearing, or worse, telling. The man who hires a caterer has hired a caterer, not a gossip columnist.)

I think the most interesting thing about my catering business—and probably the only reason I'm writing about it in some detail—is the realization that I developed some prejudice *against* my fellow blacks. I recognize, now, that this was the case, and I have berated myself for it and overcome it, but the following details will show you how easy it is for prejudice to subtly creep into a man's heart.

As I said, I sensed my customers' preference for Negroes, so I was in the habit of hiring an all-Negro staff. As time went on, some of my workers became extremely good at their jobs; they were tactful and they were efficient and highly competent. As is only natural with people who learn quickly and master their work, the time comes when they feel they can run the business as well or better than the owner and, if they express these feelings to the owner, the owner will usually resent it and eventually there is a parting of the ways. The bright employee gets fired and goes off on his own and, this, essentially, is the way most self-owned businesses get started. In America, this is called capitalism and the free enterprise system. It's as natural as apple pie.

Unfortunately, I thought of it as a distasteful, arrogant trait in black men—exclusively in black men. And that, dear reader, is prejudice.

Harboring this notion, I started to add white men to my staff, and what do you think began to happen?

You guessed it. As soon as some of these men became proficient in their job, they'd lose a little interest, be too sure of themselves, and then start to tell me what I should charge, what jobs I should or shouldn't take, and, generally, advise me how to run my business. It was the same story all over again.

This experience taught me how easy it is for people to conceive such weird prejudices and ideas about the races. I had always considered myself to be the model of the freethinker, a tolerant, patient person who saw each man, black and white, as an individual. And yet, I had fallen into the trap myself. I had classified Negroes in a certain category—a whole race of people. It was prejudice and intolerance at its best, and it was based on ignorance.

6 And they lived happily ever after

At this stage in my life, I have a son entering college, another in the sixth grade, and two daughters in junior high school. I have no doubt that all of my children will go on to college and, in their individual ways, find their share of the future and contribute something to it. The schools my children attend are good ones, without racial problems, and my youngsters have grown up in an atmosphere very much like the one I experienced as a boy. I have wanted it that way for them. It's important for young people to find out who they really are, and this is impossible in an atmosphere that is in a constant state of turmoil. Nothing robs a child of *himself* faster than being placed in an environment that demands his attention. In other words, if a young person has to spend his time coping with a neighborhood of fear and violence, he has no time to sit back quietly and reflect on just who he is, what he wants, and where he should go in the future.

This is the opportunity I have given my children, and I believe it is a priceless heritage. I don't promise that they will live happily ever after, but they have a chance to try.

We continue to enjoy our country home, and although our seclusion is not what it used to be, the white neighbors we have acquired couldn't be more pleasant. All in all, our lot in life is a satisfying one.

When the publishers asked me to contribute my story to this book, the key element they were looking for was an exposition of my attitudes—the philosophies and feelings with which I approached life and which enabled me to find a high degree of happiness in a predominantly white society.

I have mentioned a few of these attitudes, and now, in ending my story, I'd like to ramble a little bit further . . . just a few notes and comments on current issues and problems. These will be truths that I have found to exist. You may find otherwise, but, anyway, here are some final thoughts.

Ambivalence—that strange state of mind that finds a person attracted toward something, and, at the same time, repelled by it—is common to all men. It is a good trait, because it tells a man, from the day he can first understand the simplest thing, that there are always two sides to every question and to every affair in which men get themselves involved. Nothing is cut and dried. Nothing is simple. Nothing is either black or white. If a man wants to lash out at a supposed enemy, something else inside of him makes him hate the thought. The wise man recognizes this contest going on in his mind, and he stops and considers it, carefully weighing both sides, before he acts. Probably he will compromise, neither killing his supposed enemy, nor running away from him—and it is this compromise action on which all of civilization has been constructed. Without it, we would all be predatory animals, acting on first impulses and strewing chaos behind us.

I read, lately, that a Negro leader had occupied a church, broken up a religious service and demanded financial retribution from the parishioners for past injustices. In effect, he was saying, "Pay me for past injustices. Pay me for the humiliation you have caused my people." It seemed as if he were stripping the issue of its morality and saying that everything that had been done to our people was acceptable, except that they had been denied materialistic and financial gain—and payment in money would now make up for it. I find myself in sympathy with the black community's need for money, but it is difficult for me to condone the above approach when it involves a religious institution. Let the militants seek their money from American business and government, if they feel the need of retribution. Appealing for a new morality and spirit within the churches of America is a slow, discouraging process, but, in the long run, it will be more important than money, and the two issues should not be confused.

Black is the color of *our* skin. White is the color of *their* skin. When this becomes the *only* recognized difference between the white man and the black man, then brotherhood will be ushered in. Today, in the minds of many whites, blackness means slowness, apathy, irresponsibility, unpredictableness, untrustworthiness, and a host of other degrading, and untrue, characteristics. Tomorrow, when blackness means only blackness, without any further qualification, then Martin Luther King's dream will have become a reality.

And that "tomorrow" is coming. A year ago, I walked into a bank and saw a Negro at a teller's cage, and I noticed it, and I felt happy for the man. Today, I walked into a bank and hardly noticed three Negroes behind the teller's cages. Yesterday, a Negro in a white business was conspicuous. Today, it is conspicuous if there *aren't* any Negroes to be seen. Something would seem to be missing. The *lack* of Negroes in the business world would be odd and noticeable.

So, the racial situation is changing.

As a boy, I could not identify with schoolbooks. All the characters were white. Dick was white. Jane was white. As I grew up, I could not identify with all-white television commercials and advertisements, or even with baseball teams until Jackie Robinson broke the color line. And then, how I cheered for the Brooklyn Dodgers —and so did the entire black community!

Personally, I may not have liked Jackie Robinson, but that was not the point. Here was a Negro on a baseball team and, all of a sudden, it meant something to me. It could happen to me, too. It was realistic.

I try not to recognize a color line, and, therefore, white people seldom recognize the color line when they deal with me. If I am not conscious of it, and simply present myself as another American with certain talents and attributes, I find that the white man accepts it. If I am conscious of being a Negro, that feeling will show itself in my dealings, and the person with whom I'm dealing will become conscious of it himself. We will not get very far together.

I feel toward the white man the way I want him to feel toward me. I don't mind his being white, with a history of prejudice and discrimination in his society. By the same token, I don't expect him to care about my being black, with whatever he may think that implies. He's a man and I'm a man. Let's get on with business.

I think it is easy to understand people—except through their words.

The black community is divided on the issue of violence.

Violence calls attention to the black man's plight, accomplishes immediate results, because of the fear it throws into the white population, and violence is something the white man understands and respects—so goes the argument in favor of violence. And it is claimed by all its practitioners that as soon as the necessity for violence ends, violence will stop and peace will reign.

I cannot accept it. To me, violence is anathema.

I understand the frustration of a poverty-stricken black man who may lose control and strike out at authority, perhaps breaking a window and stealing a television set or some other merchandise that he can barter for food and money. I can understand how a black man could be so degraded and so outraged by blatant discrimination that, in a moment of desperation, he burns down a factory, or burns up his own block so that his miserable neighborhood has to be rebuilt. I don't agree with these actions, but they can be understood, and much is currently being done, via self-help and job-training programs, to alleviate the reasons for such action.

But what I cannot understand is the toleration of vicious groups who openly train young blacks to kill, burn, rape, steal, and to hate "whitey" and all white authority. Violent black militancy is a Frankenstein, and I lay the blame partly at the feet of moderate Negro leaders who have allowed—and tacitly condone—this anarchy in our midst. They were the parents, and they have allowed their rebellious children to run wild.

Because violent black extremists have dramatically "called attention" to the problems of blacks, anti-black prejudices have been rekindled, and may, if not checked by sensible white and black leaders, erase a generation of American progress. It is one thing for Negroes to be the object of violence, as were Martin Luther King's followers in the South, and then use eyewitness accounts of this violence to show the nation the brutality of white supremacists. A nation was stunned by what they saw— stunned into action on behalf of blacks.

It is quite another thing for the Negro to be violent himself, stunning the nation with *his* brutality and driving the nation to action *against* blacks!

In what way is an arrogant black extremist less despicable than an arrogant white policeman in Mississippi?

It was only by the barest breath—by the thinnest of possibilities—that a reluctant America began to overturn two centuries of discrimination and legally and spiritedly start to free the black man from his bonds. And it was because this nation saw dogs being set on black children and singing black marchers. A country's conscience was appalled.

How then—by what devilish reasoning!—did it now seem circumspect to black leaders to allow black extremists to burn, loot, steal, kill, and prove to this country that it need not be bothered by conscience at all?

And what is this nonsense about violence dying out when there is no longer a "need" for it? What black extremist, with a torch in one hand and a gun in the other, trained from his youth to despise white men, is suddenly going to become a peaceful citizen when someone tells him there is no longer a need for his services? Is this like the Army—where men are removed from the battle zone and sent home to a totally different environment . . . where they are removed from their former enemies, and from animosities, and can turn their attention to other things?

The violent black militant's motive is revolution. It is my fervent hope that moderate black leaders will brand the black extremists for what they are—as white extremists have been branded for what they are. Our nation has progressed too far in the last decade for responsible men to allow a return to the dark days when masses of citizens are judged by the actions of a few misfits.

Negro college students demand separate facilities. So did the South for two hundred years.

I understand the Negro's problems, and I have sympathy for them, but I vote as a citizen, not strictly as a Negro. I do not care for Mr. Nixon's slowing down integration in the South, or wooing Wallace voters via Mr. Agnew. I don't fully trust the man. But I agree with his economic views, the desperate need to halt inflation, and with many other matters that affect the country as a whole.

Ambivalency again.

I cannot condone any theory that separates the races. I am not in favor of "Black Power," or of anything that polarizes our peoples. Again, this is what the South did.

I believe this is one country, and that Negroes are a part of it, and that they will rise on talent, ambition, foresight, good sense and on other qualities that traditionally pay off in a free society. I would be as suspect of an all-black business as I would be of an all-white business. This is not the system, or the philosophy, that should be prevalent in this country.

If today's student's have any hope whatsoever, it will be that they will overcome the permissiveness of school administrators.

If my ideas sound more like those of a white man than a black man, think a little further. My ideas are simply those of a man, neither white nor black. You may agree or disagree with my ideas, but they are not necessarily representative of a race. They are representative of me.

I think that is what my story is all about.

Charles T. Brooker

FROM NOWHERE TO SOMEWHERE...
TO NOWHERE

1 City of Brotherly Love

Oog, myself and a couple of dubs (friends) decided to
skip school and take a walk in the park one day. We
were about twelve or thirteen at the time. Most of the
dubs had mothers who worked, so they didn't go to
school, except on rare occasions. My mother had to be
different and stay home where she could keep an eye
on me, so I had to wait for the right opportunities to
come along before I could cut classes. On this particular
day, there was plenty of opportunity. The Art Class was
having a cultural "outing" at the Philadelphia Museum
of Art, and it wasn't any trouble at all to split when we
got there, because a couple of hundred other cats from

several schools were wandering up and down the halls and nobody knew where anybody was. My dubs were waiting for me outside on the steps, and off we headed for the park.

It was one of those typically beautiful days in Philadelphia; the smog hung low, about second-story height, and the dirt blew down the streets, stinging your eyes and coating everything gray. Just the day for a walk along the bridle paths and among the gardens.

Anyway, we came to a place in the park where there was a waterfall, and Oog related a story about some whiteys throwing some black cats over the falls. We discussed it for a few minutes, beginning to feel a little uneasy, because we had climbed over a terrace, where people were supposed to stand and watch the falls, and had jumped down on the rocks. If those whiteys came along, we only had two choices: to jump over the falls or be thrown over. Naturally, we decided to get back up on the bridle path.

We hadn't gone more than a few feet down the path when Oog happened to glance up toward a rock outcropping and saw some whiteys running along the top. They were about our age.

"Do you see what I see?" asked Oog.

"Doesn't mean a thing to me," I said, trying to be brave for both of us.

I noticed, however, that the four of us were walking a little faster than we had before, especially when we saw another group of whiteys on some rocks on the other side of the path. By the time we reached a clearing—maybe three or four minutes after we first spotted these cats—they were converging on us and we started to run like hell.

Now, if you were black, and if you lived in the ghetto when I did, the last thing you did was ask a white cop for help. But we were desperate that day, and, all of a sudden, right in front of us, we saw a park guard.

"Mister," we said, running up to the guard out of breath, "those cats are going to beat us up!"

"What do you want me to do about it?" he said.

We should have known better, and we shouldn't have been surprised, but I remember that all of us were shocked. In about two seconds, we stood a good chance of having our heads broken, and it was clear as crystal to that guard, but he wasn't going to lift a finger.

As soon as the whiteys realized the guard wasn't going to do anything about the situation, they lit into us with rocks. They didn't even wait for the guard to go away. Three of us were pretty fast on our feet and managed to get out of there with only a few cuts and bumps, but the fourth member of our group was slow—too slow. The last we saw of him, several guys were on him and he was being badly beaten. We didn't have enough nerve to go back and help—something I remember with shame to this day.

When we knew we were safe, we slowed down and paced ourselves to arrive home about the time school let out. A half hour later, our slow dub came back and if he'd asked us to stand still so he could smash hell out of us, we would have let him. He was in bad shape and we felt like just what we were—traitors and cowards.

Later that afternoon, our differences forgotten for the moment, a bunch of us, including myself and the other dubs who had been in the park, sat around on a door-stoop talking over the day's events, and we got angrier and angrier. Five of us—Oog, Goat, Check, Don Juan and myself—decided to take an oath that we would stab the first whitey we saw, so we broke up and went home to get knives. I think I got a penknife. The other dubs had fancier stuff, like switchblades and sheath knives. As soon as we were armed, we stepped back into the shadows alongside the buildings and began our wait.

In fifteen minutes or so, two young whiteys came bicycling down the street dumb and happy, and Oog and Goat ran out and grabbed them.

"We got 'em!" yelled Oog. "Come on! We'll hold 'em and you stab 'em!"

"You got to stab 'em, yourself!" I yelled back.

Well, we couldn't stand there in the middle of the street and argue about it at the top of our lungs, so Oog and Goat cut the cats—on the thigh and on the arm, I remember—and left them lying there in the street.

We ran away, of course, and as soon as Oog could get me alone, he called me a punk and told me the time to fulfill my part of the oath would come. It was getting late by this time, however, and all of us were getting a little chicken. We knew the cops would be called by somebody when the white cats were found, so we decided to give things up for that night.

Another typical day came to a close.

2   *The Moroccos*

When my father first came to Philadelphia—long before I was born—he worked for a white landscaping contractor. He loved the work, respected his boss, and, between them, they won some blue ribbons for horticulture at the annual Convention Hall exhibits. The contractor's business went downhill sometime during my early years, and Dad would work for him on weekends to help him out, but it was tough going financially and he eventually got a job with the Philadelphia Housing Authority where he still works after twenty-five years.

My mother would do some housecleaning for other folks once in a while, but my father was a steady provider and I can't say we ever really lacked anything. We were on relief for less than a year, during a time when half the families in our neighborhood didn't have enough to eat, so I don't count that as a failure on my Dad's part. For a black man with a seventh-grade education, he did all right by my mother, my younger sister (Doris), and myself. We ate. We had decent clothes. And we lived in a warm house.

So, how come I was always in some kind of trouble?

Well, I'll tell you . . . it was impossible to avoid trouble where I lived. You didn't have to look for it. You might not even want it. It just sort of came around every corner and said hello to you. For example, it could start at a swimming pool and, before you knew it, your whole future life was charted out for you.

The particular swimming pool I'm referring to was located at the Francisville Playground in Philadelphia and my buddies and I would spend a lot of time there in the summer. About the time we were fourteen, we began to notice girls, and we also began to notice that cats from other neighborhoods liked to manhandle the chicks in *our* neighborhood. We didn't have any gangs around to stop them, and they just helped themselves. My neighborhood, as they say, was "open turf."

One afternoon, I walked home from the pool with a close friend of mine and we went to his house to cop something to eat. When we got in the door, we found a cat from another area manhandling his sister.

This was too much for my buddy. He blew his mind, grabbed something heavy, and busted the guy's head up pretty badly. The cat had to be taken to the hospital. The only reason the cops weren't called in was because of the unwritten code among blacks to keep the cops out of it. This code applied to both parties —the one being injured and the one doing the injuring.

After this experience, we knew we had to organize a gang. We weren't worried so much about keeping the chicks in our neighborhood safe; we were worried about keeping ourselves safe. The cat who was busted up was from another area that had a gang and there was no doubt in our minds that they'd be over in our territory right away to balance things up. We didn't waste any time in rounding up as many guys as we could, who felt the way we did, and we held a meeting and formed a gang, calling ourselves the "Moroccos." To make our gang look bigger than it was, we spread the word around that a local baseball team, the Royal Tigers, was a part of it. These were older cats, and, for a while, they let us get away with the deception—at least until the fighting started getting fierce. After a couple of tough encounters, the Royal Tigers drifted away, leaving the Moroccos on their own, but we had gained some valuable time and experience. Most of us in the Moroccos were around fourteen years old and we were facing gangs of guys who were a lot older, bigger and tougher.

Our territory, if you can call it that, started out mighty small—anything we could hold for a few minutes. As we learned how to fight better, our territory spread to several blocks, and it was grudgingly admitted by other gangs that the Moroccos were worth noticing— small, maybe, but tough. We didn't get this reputation by being powerhouses. We got it by using our brains.

There was one night, for example, when another Morocco and I were caught walking in an adjoining territory. There were about eight or nine guys in the other group, so instead of dusting us off, they decided they'd have a little sport. They wanted to play. So, they came up to us and started talking.

Well, these guys were older and they'd been on the wine a little bit. They were clumsy. And what they didn't know was that Tommy, the leader of the Moroccos, was walking about fifteen yards behind us. Tommy saw what was happening, and while these cats were having their sport with us, he took the time to look around the place and pick up some bottles and bricks. When he was ready, he yelled out to one of the guys: "Okay, go ahead and do what you're gonna do. I got ten more Moroccos back here and we're comin' at you!"

Then he started throwing the bottles and bricks into the group, and my buddy and I slid (punched unexpectedly) a couple of the guys and got out of there.

It was things like that that kept us alive in those early days.

These fights I'm talking about were strictly blacks against blacks. We never had racial gang fights, and the closest thing I can remember to something like that happened this way:

For some reason, tension with whitey in our area had been getting pretty tight. The white guys had to come over to black territory to go to school and use the playground and some skirmishes had occasionally broken out—nothing serious, but things were tense and some of the older people were afraid a real race riot was in the making. The principal characters in this drama, if I remember correctly, were Ducky, a black cat, and Spanish Otty, a white cat. These guys were in their late teens, both of them were really tough, and they had a lot of guys who would fight for them. They'd been throwing insults at each other from long range for a few months and each of them figured he was tougher than the other one.

To head off major trouble, the older people suggested that these two cats fight it out alone. The word was passed on to Spanish Otty, but there wasn't any answer, so the racial tensions stayed red hot. The lid almost came off when it was rumored one afternoon that Spanish Otty and a couple of hundred whites were on their way to the playground to settle things. I was pretty young at the time, but I was at the playground and I know there must have been at least five hundred blacks milling around, waiting for Spanish Otty and his boys to come across Fairmount Avenue. Philadelphia didn't know it, but the city was on the verge of open warfare.

With everyone concentrating on Fairmount Avenue, nobody paid any attention to a panel truck that slowly drove up into the middle of the playground and stopped. The back doors swung open—and out stepped Spanish Otty and one of his brothers.

You can believe he didn't stay unnoticed for long, and, in a few seconds, a crowd was around him and I remember how quiet everything was. The crowd was surprised—stunned, I think—by Spanish Otty's guts, and they waited for him to speak.

He stood on the step by the back door of the panel truck and said: "All I want is the baddest black man that's out here, whoever he may be."

The crowd remained silent for a few more moments, and then somebody said, "Okay, let's have the fight."

Spanish Otty beat Ducky pretty badly—there's no sense going into details—and then got back in the truck and drove way. Just like that. It was simple and fast.

There wasn't even time for the crowd to react. The threat of a big race riot was all over, and the people went home.

Naturally, Ducky didn't feel any too happy about being beaten up in front of five hundred blacks, and it was reported that later that night he went looking for Spanish Otty and beat him in a fair fight.

I don't know. I didn't see this second fight, and the way it was talked about, I doubt that it happened. It was just one of those things I'll never know.

One thing I do know, is that in all the street fights we had in those days, I only heard of one cat being killed. I wasn't there at the time, and the Moroccos weren't involved in it, but, as I look back, I think it is a miracle that half of us aren't dead.

3   The All-American cat

The All-American cat—that was me. A confirmed wino at fifteen, and while other guys carried books to school, I carried a half-pint bottle of wine, a knife and a list of girls who were "willing."

I never told my mother anything. She was strict, and my buddies hated to face her when I got drunk in school, or after school, and had to be carried home. So they'd take me to the door, prop me up against the moulding, knock on the door and run. When my mother opened the door, I'd crumble onto the floor and lie there smiling at her. This was pretty rough on my mother, but I was "nobody" if I didn't have a bottle of wine in school, and to be a student at Ben Franklin High School without another essential item—a knife— was plain suicide.

You see, after each summer was over, especially when the gang fighting had been really bitter, everybody was afraid to go to school. There was a lot of resentment and everybody was up tight. The Moroccos weren't the big daddies in Ben Franklin yet, so we, of all the cats, had to skip school a few weeks in September to let things cool down. If we'd set foot in school, we would have been greased by members of the rival gangs.

Well-meaning people still tell me today that my background was underprivileged, and that's why I got into so much trouble. I agree with them, and that's what I tell the police and judges and anyone else. It comes in handy sometimes as an excuse.

Anyway, I managed to stay out of school until about the last week in September one year, when my mother finally put her foot down and made me go. I took my knife and bottle of wine, to give me courage, and went to good old Ben Franklin.

The rival gang members didn't give a damn about teachers, cops, or anyone—they really controlled the school—so when they heard I was in school, their warlord stopped me in the hall and told me that, when I came out of class, his gang would be waiting for me.

I knew what the score was.

"There's no gettin' away today," the warlord said. "You have to get your ass kicked today. That's all there is to it."

So—I took my place in the classroom. I guess I was supposed to study. A few minutes later, the door opened and the warlord stepped into the room. He wasn't satisfied with just giving me a warning in the hall. He wanted to be sure I dug him.

The teacher looked at the warlord and said, "Are you in this class?" As far as I knew, this guy wasn't even a student.

"Just go on with your studies and we won't bother you," said the warlord. (I can't remember this guy's name, so I have to keep calling him "warlord.")

"You have no business in here," said the teacher. "Get out!"

"You're my business," said the warlord, pointing to me. "And you're my business," he said again, pointing to my buddy, Charlie, "I'll see you when you come out."

The cat leaves, and Charlie and I looked at each other. Then we quietly closed our books, got up and started walking toward the door.

"Sit down!" screams the teacher, but we didn't pay any attention. We knew we had to go down the hall to another classroom and pick up Charlie's older brother. We needed all the help we could get.

After getting Charlie's brother, Jim—we just walked in and told him to come with us—we held a strategy conference in the hall. We knew there was no way out of the school; the other gang had every exit covered. So, we decided it would be better to get greased on a side street, rather than on Broad Street, so we headed for the back exit, and, sure enough, there was a bunch of cats waiting for us at the bottom of the stairs. We stood on the landing and looked down at them.

"We finally got ya!" said one of the guys, smiling up at us casually. "Come on down. You may as well get it over with."

We were about ready to start down the steps and take our chances, when the exit door opened and Tommy, the leader of the Moroccos, stepped in—with a gun in his hand!

Tommy came strolling in through the crowd, waving the gun in their faces and smiling. "Now, what did you say was gonna happen?" he asked them. Then he smashed a couple of them and tweaked their noses and told them that what they had in mind for us wasn't nice.

Then he looked up at us in mock surprise and said, "What are you cats standing up there for? Come on down here."

On the way down the steps, we slid a couple of the guys and called them punks, and then we walked out the door as big as life. We wished we'd had a car, because we felt pretty big.

We were still in enemy territory, of course, and a lot of cats from the other gang were following us.

"Just take it easy," advised Tommy, holding the gun in plain sight. "Don't run, whatever you do. Just keep your head."

When we were about two blocks away from the school, Jim, Charlie and I couldn't stand it any longer and we broke out in a run for our home territory. About an hour later, when we saw Tommy again, he was angry as hell.

"You guys will never be worth a damn," he said, disgustedly. And I guess we knew then we weren't going to be the really tough cats we hoped to be.

The reason Tommy had appeared at the school exit with a gun, and saved us at the last minute, like the cavalry in cowboy pictures, was because he'd been at the movies and met some dubs who told him my mother had made me go to school.

"Dumb Ass!" said Tommy. And he rushed out of the movie, went home for his gun, and had been walking around the school, inspecting the exits, when we appeared. He really saved our asses.

I didn't go to school for two weeks—you can believe it—but the time came when I couldn't intercept *every* letter that came from the school, and my mother finally got wise and sent me back to "study."

Nobody could really study in that school, of course. Everything was a fight for survival. If you were dumb enough to take your lunch to the cafeteria, somebody stole it. If you got a portion of it, it was only because the bigger cats were taking it easy on you. This went for white as well as black students.

Take the fire tower at the school for example. Ben Franklin High School was built like a medieval castle, and an emergency fire stairway wound its way from top to bottom. This "fire tower," as they called it, was exclusively the property of blacks. Some were students, and some weren't. It didn't make any difference. Only blacks were allowed in this fire tower, and any whitey who tried to use it would have had to be insane.

I remember one incident that happened after my gym class. The idea was to skip my shower and head for the fire tower for a crap game and a swig of wine, which I did, and as I was running down the stairs at the fourth floor level, I saw a whitey getting it pretty badly. Well, there was nothing I could do about it. I just stepped over him—but I could hear him screaming all the way down to street level.

You might not believe it—or maybe you would— but some of the more militant guys even held pistol practice in the fire tower. You'd think the noise would bring the cops, but nothing like that ever happened that I recall. The teachers were helpless, of course, and with such chaos going on all the time, the only way any of us could pass our grades was to cheat. I was good at cheating. What else could I do? I couldn't study.

All the way through high school I knew the only way to make it on the outside was to hustle. My mother and father might not have agreed, but I was considered a hip cat. I knew what was out there. If I stole or wrote numbers . . . this was all there was. My only thought beyond high school was the same as everybody else's:

someday I'd see a bank truck rolling down the street with a lot of money in it, and if the right cats were around to help me, we'd knock it off and be set for the rest of our lives. And if we got caught, so what? What's ten years in jail when the only other thing to do is stand around on the street corner? I never had a thought about being a doctor or a lawyer or an Indian chief or anything. The only thing they encouraged us to be in school was an auto mechanic, and that wasn't for me. I guess I'd been in the school counselor's office fifteen times, and every time he'd say, "You ought to be an auto mechanic, Charlie." After a while, I knew the *last* thing I'd ever be was an auto mechanic. That counselor was like a broken record.

My sister, Doris, on the other hand, was a good, steady student. To show you the contrast between us, Doris was president and valedictorian of her junior high school graduating class, and I think she was also valedictorian of her senior high school graduating class. Doris went to an all-girl high school and I went to an all-boy high school. They were sister and brother schools and my sister and I were the only students in either school with the same last name. Do you know, that in four years, the teachers *never* realized we were brother and sister. They never related the names—there was that big a difference between her character and mine.

A typical example of why it never crossed the teachers' minds that a guy like me could be related to somebody as nice and bright as Doris happened in the school hallway one day. I'm pretty small—only five-foot-three, today—and this big cat from South Philadelphia needed a victory, I guess, so he decided to pick on me.

I was pretty good in those days and I could usually make a big guy look bad. Maybe I wouldn't always beat him, but I'd always come close enough to make the other cats laugh at him. Anyway, I started getting the best of this cat and he pulled out a knife just as a teacher came by. Somehow, the teacher got us to stop fighting and took us down to the counselor's office. The counselor took one look at me, and, knowing my reputation as a troublemaker, called the juvenile authorities. Remember, I hadn't started this fight, and, to be honest, the last thing I ever did in that school was *make* trouble. I spent those four years trying to *avoid* trouble. But— my reputation was as a troublemaker, and that was that.

So, two big detectives came in and took me down the steps of the school and put me in a squad car and drove me downtown. They questioned me, and thinking the worst about everything, gave me an examination for syphilis and who the hell knows what else. It was a bad experience. My father had to come down and get me, and the way he stared at me was worse than if he'd beaten me.

And so it went during my high school days. One thing I'm proud of is that I always paid my way. I worked in a lamp factory after school, swept out a garage and did other odd jobs. Add the profits from a few things I stole now and then and I never had to count on help from anyone.

I was the all-American cat working his way through high school.

4 / *Whitey*

I mentioned earlier that the Moroccos never tangled with white gangs as far as I could remember, and that the whole white-black situation was never a real "thing" with us in those days. Oh, we had our thoughts on the subject, and I'll get into that later, but, aside from the fight with the whiteys in the park when I was twelve (the fight I ran away from), there are only a couple of other minor white-black instances I was involved in, personally.

Our neighborhood was about evenly divided between whites and blacks, and that was a good thing. No group could really muster an overwhelming advantage and jump on the other group. This fifty-fifty balance kept things pretty quiet. However, I learned early that a whitey in uniform, like that park guard who wouldn't help us, wasn't anyone to be trusted, and about the only other racial-type instances I was involved in were with white men in uniform.

I had an uncle who I guess you could say was something like the town drunk. He'd sleep it off anywhere he could . . . doorways, sidewalks, it didn't matter, and this one afternoon he decided to catch up on his sleep in an empty lot adjoining our house.

Well, a white cop was on the beat and I suppose it was his job to get the drunks off the street—or off empty lots—and he came over and shook my uncle and woke him up. Roused out of his sleep, and probably still half out of it, my uncle began to give him some lip, and the cop allowed as how he was going to crack my uncle's skull if he didn't shut up and do as he was told. I'm sure the cop didn't mean it . . . it was just part of the general process of getting drunks moving.

In the meantime, I was watching all of this over the backyard fence. I was about five years old, and with me was our family's big German Shepherd. My uncle loved this dog, and the dog thought my uncle was God, and it so happened that the fence between my uncle and the dog was just high enough so that when the cop started grappling with my uncle the dog could stand up on his hind feet and look over.

Well, with a little help from me, one of the boards in the fence came loose and that dog came out of the yard like he'd been let loose from a fiery furnace and, in full flight, he caught that cop about chest high and sent him cartwheeling.

The next thing I know, the cop was standing there with a drawn pistol, pointing it at the dog, and hollering: "I'm going to shoot both of you black bastards if somebody doesn't get this dog out of here!"

It was complicated. My uncle was staggering around, just trying to keep his footing and focus on something steady. The dog was standing between him and the cop. I was running across the yard to get the dog, and my mother was screaming from the upstairs window for me to stay out of it.

The way it all worked out was that somehow we managed to get the dog back in the yard—and that wasn't as easy as it sounds—and the cop took my uncle off to jail, muttering to himself about the kind of fate that would force him to work in such a neighborhood.

It was a minor incident—you know—but it left a bad taste in my mouth for white men in uniforms.

Then there's the story about Big Red. This was a white cop we all hated. He was really hard on black cats, and we stayed up late at nights figuring out how to get rid of this guy without having to kill him—a thought that crossed our minds on several occasions. The main reason we hated him was because he wouldn't let us do what we wanted to do, like raise hell, steal a little bit and things like that.

We were in high school at the time, and a couple of the dubs in our group were smart—these were the guys we left alone and allowed to study so we could copy their papers. They suggested we get up a petition to have Big Red removed from the corner.

You know, we got a *thousand* signatures on that petition.

We took the petition to City Hall, and, sure enough, they assigned Big Red to another part of the city. After that, we used to greet each other with the words, "Where's Big Red?"

Another incident with a *near*-white man in uniform

(you'll see what I mean in a moment) happened when I was in high school and went with some younger cats to play basketball at the junior high school one night.

While I was innocently shooting baskets, my gang, the Moroccos, was in the process of shooting up a guy's house. I still don't know what the beef was about, but some of the cats in the Moroccos wanted this other guy pretty badly and they'd found some rifles somewhere and were systematically shooting his house to pieces.

I didn't know about it that night, and I still didn't know about it in school the next day. When I came home from school, however, I saw my mother standing on the steps and I knew something was wrong. Usually, when I came home from school, I'd change my clothes, but this time my mother just told me to put the books down and go with her.

"Where we going?" I asked her. "You gonna buy me something new or something?"

"Shut up and don't be so smart," she said. So I shut up.

She took me to the police station at tenth and Buttonwood, and there were all the guys from the Moroccos. I wasn't allowed to talk or anything, so I just sat there without the slightest idea of what was going on.

About a half hour later, my father comes in, and by this time one of the detectives had started questioning me about the shooting and I'm beginning to put the pieces together. My father stood there a moment, listening to the questioning, and then he walked up to the head detective and asked him if he could speak with him privately for a minute.

"Look, just sit down and wait," said the detective, annoyed. "We'll get to you. Your boy's nothing special. He won't get any privileges."

"I just want five minutes, that's all," my father said.

Maybe my father said something else, I don't know, but he and the detective went off in a corner and talked. When the detective came back, he seemed like a changed man. He said to me: "You say you weren't with them?"

I said, "That's right."

"You say you can prove it?" he asked.

"Yeah, I can prove it."

"Well, you don't look like you belong with these other punks."

"Yes, sir," I said, "not me."

"Okay," said the detective, "I've had a talk with your father and you can go. Get out of here."

I didn't say anything to my father on the way home, and I didn't feel like eating dinner. I waited until my father was finished and then I asked him what he'd told the detective.

"I recognized that detective when I walked in the room," said my father. "We used to pick cotton together when we were boys in the South. He's black, passing for white—and all I did was remind him of our past friendship. He told me I had the wrong guy, but I told him his mother's name, and his father's name and his sister's name, and so on, until he admitted I knew him."

"And then what?" I asked.

"Nothing. I told him I didn't care what he was doing, but I wanted him to give you a break. I heard your story and I knew you weren't involved in the shooting. That's all."

And that *was* all.

I had told the truth and had earned the rewards of the innocent. It was only right.

5 Big man off campus

My graduation from high school was as memorable for me as for anyone else. My mother bought me a new suit that was two sizes too big for me, some dubs bought me two fifths of wine, and I got bombed out of my skull in a hoagie shop.

It was beautiful.

As I was feeling my way for the door at the hoagie shop, with some idea in mind of going over to a chick's house, six or seven cats from out of town spotted me and asked me to settle an argument for them. The reputation of the Moroccos was sky-high at this time, and so was mine, and even these strangers to the neighborhood had been told about us—so, they asked my advice.

I listened to the arguments, decided in favor of one

side, and then, feeling like wise King Solomon, strutted off to see my chick. A couple of hours later, with an additional fifth of wine in me, I was weaving my way back up the street, and who should be waiting for me but the guys I had decided against—two or three of them as I remember, although I was in no condition to remember very much.

They really smashed me, flattening me out on the sidewalk and then, when they figured I must be dead, they rolled me off into the gutter.

I wasn't dead. I don't think I was really even hurt. For all I know, I could have been lying there, at eye level with the curb, laughing my brains out as I felt my jaw to see how many teeth I had left. (Today, I have seven teeth, which is pretty good for my old crowd.) It goes without saying that those strangers left the neighborhood fast. The Moroccos would have taken a dim view of their anti-social actions.

As I mentioned a moment ago, the reputation of the Moroccos advanced considerably. By the time I graduated from high school, our territory had doubled and tripled and, although we were generally liked in the neighborhood, we began to enjoy our power and act like the other gangs we had been fighting. We weren't above a little oppression now and then, and a lot of other guys paid tribute to us in the form of wine and other useful commodities. When the Moroccos raised hell, we did it outside of our own neighborhood, so people didn't know about most of our scrapes with the law. Actually, there weren't too many other gangs who would tangle with us, so, just to keep things lively, we eventually got to the point where we'd fight among ourselves. I suppose you could say that during those first few years after my graduation, the Moroccos were a social club. Our primary motive in life was to throw parties and mess up chicks—and this we did with talent and dedication.

As for me, I was putting my education to use and working as a laborer in a lamp factory. I was still waiting for the "big deal" to come along.

Two years after graduation, my father asked me to help him build a house on a lot he had purchased in the country. Even though he said he'd pay me for my help, his proposition threatened to restrict my social life considerably. What he had in mind was that I would come home from the lamp factory at my usual time, five o'clock, eat between five and five-thirty, and then we'd all happily drive out to the country and work on his house until midnight or something. Not only that, but my father thought it would be nice if I also helped him on Saturdays and Sundays.

Well, he was my father. And there was my mother, looking forward to that house in the country as if it were the Promised Land. So what could I do? I helped him. I helped him every evening and I helped him on the weekends. Every once in a while, when I'd meet some gentle soul in Philadelphia, he'd say how nice it was for me to be able to get out of the city and work in the country . . . what a privilege it was to get away from all the city's dirt and trouble.

People like this were insane. The only things I was

getting away from were booze and chicks, which didn't make me a bit happy, and as far as the country was concerned, the fresh air was killing me. I hated it.

But that wasn't half as bad as lying in the hospital after an operation for kidney stones. I mean, here I had been working nights and weekends in the country, losing contact with my buddies, and now I was in a hospital for six weeks. The only thing that made life promising was that the house had been finished and when I got out of the hospital I could look forward to resuming a normal life in the city.

My recuperation period was tougher than I had expected. I was really weak. I stayed at my aunt's house, friend's houses . . . anywhere I could, and, of course, I could only work now and then. The old street fights and wounds had caught up with me, and I didn't heal like an untouched flower.

I was at my aunt's house one day when my mother made one of her infrequent visits to the city. I look pretty miserable even in the best of health, but I guess my sickened condition frightened her. She took me down to Robert Hall and bought me a winter jacket, and she gave me a couple of bucks. Then she persuaded me to come home to the house in the country until I could get my strength back and find a job.

For once, I didn't argue with her, and I lived with my folks in the country for about six months, finding a pretty good job in a local laboratory. It was an experiment for me, and, being the wise and grateful son my parents expected me to be, a son who would see how decent and clean the life was out in the country, I naturally split back to the city as soon as I was well.

I kept my job at the laboratory, however, and commuted to and from the city. Things were going well. The job paid good wages, I had a new car, good clothes and a nice chick. In short, I lived it up, and it was a wild period in my life—as wild as any I had experienced before, with plenty of "drunk and disorderly" charges laid on me, but never anything big. I never stole a car, for example, or committed a felony—it was just a crazy period, full of general hell-raising. There are a lot of details I could go into about those days, but except to say that I had a son and a stormy marriage that broke up, it's better to let things lie.

Let me put it this way: there came a time when I couldn't continue to run in high gear all the time—when I couldn't keep on wenching and boozing and pumping adrenalin into myself—a time when I had to stop and relax and find some peace. Maybe it followed a bad night of drinking, or a close call with the police, or something else that had me uptight and almost sick to my stomach. I don't know. But I do know I faced myself one morning, and my busted marriage, and my poor health and my spring-taut condition, and I told myself that I *needed* the country. If any man alive just needed some place to sit down and rest, it was me.

And I went back.

And I stayed back.

6 Two steps forward, one step backward

When I went back to the country, I won't tell you that I went back as a changed man, renouncing all my old sins, or anything like that. I was the same Charlie Brooker, just a little more relaxed, that's all. I stayed with my mother and father, but I often went back to the city and ran with the Moroccos. The main difference was that it wasn't a full-time occupation. It wasn't the central thing in my life. It was just a diversion.

And I won't say that I stayed out of trouble—but I didn't get into as much of it as before. I still held my job at the laboratories, I was married again, some children came along, and my wife and I moved into our own house in a nearby town. Many nights, some of my buddies from the Moroccos would come out and have drinks with us, and, likely as not, I would go off with them for a while.

Did I resent the intrusion? Or did I feel trapped by my past?

Never. Most of the time, I was the one who invited them up. I loved those cats . . . Shad, Oog, Fit, Pep, and everybody else I used to hang around with. Sure, my life was different now. My kids were going to decent schools. They were experiencing a better way of life. They had opportunities I never had, and their futures looked sharp. And I was happy for them.

But their old man was still the guy who was a touch on the shady side of the law. Old loyalties, memories, obligations demanded it—and, let's be honest, so did a certain carefree instinct on my own part. There is nothing brutal in me, and hurting people is not in my line, but I confess that at that time I retained an inbred interest in a little polite petty larceny now and then. Sometimes I think I would have made an accomplished politician.

We lived directly across the street from the railroad tracks, and I remember waiting for the last train to go by one night and then dropping off to sleep, and I had a dream.

The dream took me back to when I was fourteen years old, just about the time the Moroccos had been formed. The dream was true—more of a memory, really, than a dream, and it began at a party all of us in the Moroccos had attended one evening.

As the party got underway, a man—let's call him "Wicks"—came in, looked around, and started mouthing off. He was about ten years older than any of us, and he was part of the adult group in the area who suspected our Morocco gang might amount to something and throw the older guys out of power in the neighborhood. I think Wicks was afraid of not being a chief anymore.

Anyway, Wicks said, "How you punks doin'?"

Naturally, this brought a screaming halt to the festivities (we were dancing with the chicks and all of us had drinks), and, finally, one of our guys said, "The punk is you."

Well, one word led to another, and, for some reason, maybe because Wicks didn't push too hard, a fight didn't take place and the rest of the guys went back to dancing. All except me. Being small, I probably wanted to make it look like I was a big man, so I sat up on a high table and said a few words to Mr. Wicks, instead of standing where I was and keeping my mouth shut.

The next thing I knew, Wicks pulled out two ice picks and put the points up against my stomach. This was a grown man, remember.

"Look, punk," he said. "One word . . . just one word out of your big mouth and I'm gonna stick both of these in you and that will be the end."

I believed him. Man, I really believed him. I didn't even start to say anything. I just sat there breathing through my nose, and my ears and my eyes.

This went on for a couple of minutes and out of the corner of my eye I happened to see Check. Check was half blind and he couldn't see what was happening to me, but he stood six feet tall (he was fifteen) and was the hardest-hitting guy in the Moroccos. He was light skinned, with red hair, freckles and a game leg, but he was unbelievable in a fight.

By luck, another Morocco noticed my plight and whispered to Check that I was in trouble. The ice picks weren't exactly in plain sight, but there was something funny about the scene that required caution, and this other Morocco sensed it. He must have told Check to do his job with great care, because Check sidled up to Wicks as quietly as a shadow.

When Check hit him it was like a movie scene. The ice picks went flying up in the air and the punch drove Wicks clear into the other room. This was our cue to dust him off and smash hell out of him. Then Wicks jumped out the window.

About a half hour later, the front door was flung open, and there stood Wicks with a machete in his hand, inviting all the Moroccos to come outside. He was a mad, angry man.

The house in which we were having the party belonged to a veteran, and one of our guys, named Shad, pulled a bayonet off the wall and went out to meet Wicks. Shad was a quiet guy, but he was always being put in spots like this for some reason or other. He wasn't a bit angry, but there he was in a life-and-death bayonet-machete fight with a man who had a reputation for being one of the two men in town who had a submachine gun.

I hate to end the story this way—but nothing happened. Wicks and Shad sparred with each other for about five blocks. Both of them were pretty well gassed up on wine and I guess they just got tired and quit. It's an even worse ending if I tell you that most of us ended up being good friends with Wicks, but that's the way it was.

I woke up from this dream-memory and my thoughts turned to my kids in the adjoining rooms. It was quiet outside, like it is in any small town at night, and I remember thinking to myself that I was glad my kids weren't in the same atmosphere I had grown up in. I didn't want anyone punching ice picks into their stomachs.

I didn't know it, but I think this was the beginning of some serious soul-searching on my part. A transition was beginning to take place. Nothing important, yet, but something was stirring inside of me.

I think the leopard was beginning to change its spots.

7 Paradise lost

You know, it's funny how your past catches up with you at the most unexpected moments. It's like a shadow you can't run away from.

For the past few months, with things like that dream on my mind, I've been asking myself questions. The kids come home from school, they're not drunk, they're not bleeding. They've got books and they know what's in them. Most of them will probably go on to college to become tomorrow's black leaders instead of tomorrow's black convicts. When they go to school, they *learn* something. No getting their brains kicked in. No fight for survival. They've got a better chance than I had.

So, what do I tell them? Do I tell them to stand

outside on the sidewalk and wait for that stupid bank truck to come along so they can heist it and make a fortune? Do I tell them to stop reading books and *make* book instead? Do I tell them to put a gang together and beat up everybody in sight like a bunch of illiterate tribes in Africa? Do I tell them it's better to fight the establishment with bricks, rather than with brains?

What do I tell them?

To tell the truth, I've been walking around like a robot. I'm in a transition period, and it's complicated. Maybe if I were still living back in Philadelphia, and the same circumstances applied to my kids that applied to me, I'd tell them to do what I did. Only they don't live back in Philadelphia where you have to have three eyes to stay alive on your way to school in the morning. If you live in the jungle, you have to learn how to survive in the jungle. It's a full-time job. If you're lucky, and you escape from the jungle, you can turn your attention toward better things . . . toward the future.

So, the things I learned, and the things I did, don't apply to my kids. And I think that's what makes it so tough. I've given them a home in the country. I've given them that one chance in a million they need to really make it in the future. And the best thing I can do for them now is to see to it they continue to have that home . . . that nothing disrupts their big chance to stay out of the jungle.

Only I might not be able to do it. Now that it's here . . . now that I know what I must do for my family . . . now that I know the big difference between where I grew up and where my kids are growing up, and the different things they have to learn—it may be too late.

Because right now, January, 1970, I'm under $15,000 bail for conspiracy, larceny and burglary—and I may be in jail by the time you read this book!

8   *Telling it like it is*

Let's face it, I almost had it made. Little Charlie Brooker had come from nowhere to somewhere. I didn't even know it, and I don't know how I got here. Just dumb luck. I should have been dead a long time ago.

But now that I've got it, I don't want to lose it— and let me tell you why.

The coming generation will be different than my generation, and I want to be sure my kids have every opportunity to get the most they can out of our changing society. Living out here, without big-city pressures, they can find out who they are and they can figure out for themselves what is best for them. If one of my kids wants to be an auto mechanic, fine. If another one wants to be an attorney, or a civil rights worker, and learn about law, communication, and about the real sources of power in our society, and about the methods and avenues by which changes can be made, that's fine with me, too. Not everybody wants to do the same thing—but everybody should have a chance to do what he wants to do, and that's the biggest benefit a home like mine can give young people. That's the reason I want to keep it.

My kids will face plenty of pressures when they're older—and that's soon enough—because we still live in an unjust, violent society, and it will take more violence to change it. Martin Luther King knew this when he sent his marchers down those Mississippi roads. He knew his people would be attacked by dogs, beaten by cops, hosed down, sprayed with tear gas, and would have their homes and churches bombed. King wasn't stupid. He knew exactly what was going to happen—violence, and lots of it. His speeches prepared his followers for the violence he knew was going to come, and, when it did come, and the TV cameras were there to record it, he turned the results of the violence against the whites. Million of whites saw exactly what kind of brutality whites practiced.

If there hadn't been violence . . . if King's followers hadn't been stomped on and smashed to the ground, shot at and manhandled . . . then what would he have accomplished? It was the violence that aroused compassion and understanding in the hearts of many whites. King knew it. And he was right. Lots of young blacks today think of Martin Luther King as an Uncle Tom—even I thought so once—but, when you analyze it, he was as smart a leader as any. He knew the need for violence if the black man was to make progress.

The white man notices violence. It is something he

can understand. He's practiced it himself for so long, convincing his children that things are worth fighting and dying for—something you seldom hear in a black family—that violence has become the one factor in life he really recognizes and understands. We're "niggers" to a lot of whites, and no amount of quiet reasoning is going to change that impression. But if we get our heads busted in, or if we bust their heads in, the whites are suddenly aware that the black man exists and has to be reckoned with. Fortunately, somewhere in the hearts of all of us, black and white alike, is a stopping point— a barrier to all-out confrontation. None of us wants to kill all the whites or kill all the blacks, or anything of the sort. What the blacks are doing now is skirmishing . . . making the white man realize that we are here. Threats are hurled by both sides, some fighting occurs, things cool down, and then another battle erupts. People get scared and wonder what it's all coming to. The whites lock their doors, the blacks board up their windows, maybe a block gets burned; sometimes, even people get killed—but not often, and then usually by mistake.

This is the game that's going on. The blacks are screaming: "We're here, man! We're here!" The whites can't avoid noticing—they can't really close their eyes to a city block in flames, you know.

But violence, in one form or another—either actual or threatened—either direct or indirect—whether practiced by Martin Luther King or a Black Panther or a George Wallace—has been the one thing that has advertised the injustices toward the black man and given him every gain he's achieved in the last twenty years.

It's a revolution of sorts—not a revolution by the white man's standards, where they line up a couple of million men in the North and a couple of million men in the South and then slaughter each other. It's not a revolution by those standards—we don't think that way. It's a revolution that consists of hundreds of small battles—fire fights they call them in the Army—hit-and-run tactics that keep the whites aware that the black man still has a long way to go before he's really equal and before there will be peace again in this country.

Already there are some signs of change. The Black Panthers began by saying, "Hate Whitey!" This was the recruiting stage—like the Army said to "Hate Japs! Hate Germans! Hate Russians!" That sort of thing—though God knows the black man had more reason to hate—really hate—the whites than Americans ever had to hate anybody, except maybe the Japanese. After a while, "Hate Whitey!" was replaced with "Black Power"—the first stage, the hate and distrust stage, that of making sure blacks understood the problems they faced with whites, was now replaced by a black awareness.

Now another stage has started—maybe the last one. The Black Panthers are now "for the people." The cycle is being completed. First it was hate for the whites, then black awareness, and now the whites are brought back into the picture.

This doesn't mean everything has been accomplished—but it shows the general strategy behind black militancy. The cycle may have to be completed again and again, but, at its base, there is no love for violence for the sake of violence, and no long-range purpose to "take over" the country. Certain individuals may love violence, and may want to conquer the nation (there are extremists in every group), but the overall guiding principle behind the present upheaval in American society is to make it crystal clear to America that blacks are Americans and insist on being equal with their white contemporaries. There will be hell to pay until that principle is a reality—and there will be peace on the day it *is* a reality. In the meantime, the necessity for violence—whether in the Martin Luther King style, or the Black Panther style, as I said before—is the only language that whites seem to understand.

My children will have to grow up and face this sort of complicated, disruptive society—and, like many white children—it is a shame they can't simply live quiet, happy lives in a country at peace with itself and with its conscience. I wish it were different. I wish there were no need for Martin Luther Kings, or Black Panthers, or Malcolm X's. I wish there were no prejudice. No discrimination. No hate.

Thousands of blacks have gotten into trouble with the law, wrecked their futures, and have been ruined before their time just trying, in their youth, to *be* somebody . . . somebody the white society would not let them be. Somebody. *Anybody*, except a dumb, black nigger who isn't allowed to work here, or there, or to progress, or to live decently, or to make a wage comparable to that of a white man. Treated like animals, they acted like animals, and maybe the best way they could express themselves was to fight with each other on street corners and throw bricks at taxi drivers.

That's changed. It's a different, bigger, more complex struggle today, where brains, strategy and knowledge are the important credentials. And I want my kids to be prepared for it.

And I'll tell you something else, too. Every black reader of this book—there may be some exceptions, but I don't think so—knows in his soul that way down deep the thing he hates most is hate. This is a fact in the black man. Really analyze yourself and think about it— you hate hate.

The day the white man realizes this, and stops giving us reason to hate, the United States of America will be a kingdom of brotherhood and progress the like of which the world has never seen or envisioned.

I think the real, lasting hope is in the kids of today. They've grown up watching blacks and whites kick each other's brains out, hate each other, insult each other. They've been aware of the injustices, of the stupidity of the "system," of the bigotry. They've heard their parents talk about black militants, white supremacists, integration, segregation—they've seen suspicion, distrust, violence, and hypocrisy on both sides of the fence.

And they're sick to death of it.

They turn themselves off, sometimes on dope—anything to escape the insanity in men's minds and hearts. They band together for comfort. They do their own "thing." Nothing they do is half as bad as the madness practiced by their forebears.

It's so bad, really, that these kids today *have* to make it better . . . and there is hope in this simple, unavoidable fact.

Now, here's a little idea of what the world can be like—someday, someday—after the need for violence and confrontation is over, and the wounds have been healed and black and white *brothers* walk over the face of America:

I drove my oldest daughter to a graduation party at the home of one of her white friends. As I was coming around the block, a bunch of the white kids were hanging over the backyard fence. They asked me to let my daughter out right there, rather than drive around to the front of the house. I let her out, and they started laughing and pulled her over the fence, happy to have her and not thinking anything more about it. They weren't putting on a show. They were just being themselves—sincere, open, spontaneous.

It's a sign, maybe.

Give the kids time, and who knows what may happen tomorrow?

9 *Summing up*

It's a long way from where I grew up to where I am today. Maybe I don't have a mansion, but I live where I want to live and, except for my pending trial, I would say that I'm happy. When I look at my kids and consider what is, and what could have been, I don't have any complaints.

My mother and father had a lot to do with helping me get out of the slums, but self-analysis was the most important thing. I knew I wasn't really cut out for big-time hustling—that takes special talent and dedication. I didn't feel I had it, and I didn't look the part, anyway. So, if I couldn't make the big time, then what was left for me except penny-ante deals, working in a lamp factory and trying to be a big man on street corners for the rest of my life? I wanted better than that. Why not? I wasn't going to get it there, so I came out here. I settled down to work (I've had the same job for eighteen years), and I can truthfully say I would never want to go back and live in my old neighborhood again.

You see, I'm trying to be careful with what I say and not overstate it—because I don't want to sound like a preacher, and I'm not much for giving advice. I know how a lot of you feel out there, because I was there, but what's good for me might not be good for you. There are just three things I'd like to say, and I don't think this could be called preaching.

First—it's bad when blacks fight blacks. Black people have too much to cope with in our society to waste time fighting each other.

Second—if you're spirited and have an itch to get into trouble, maybe you ought to think about joining one of the militant black groups, instead of stealing hubcaps for kicks. Black people could use your energy and guts.

And third—if all you want to do is make a decent place for yourself in the world, and maybe help the black cause in quieter ways, then you'll have to do the hardest thing of all. You'll have to get a good education and really study.

That's all from Charlie Brooker.

DATE DUE

	Withdrawn From		
	Ohio Northern		
	University Library		
GAYLORD			PRINTED IN U.S.A.